A Luang Prabang Love Story

A Luang Prabang Love Story

Manisamouth
Ratana Koumphon

RIVER

BOOKS

First published and distributed in 2020 by
River Books
396 Maharaj Road, Tatien, Bangkok 10200
Tel. 66 2 622-1900, 224-6686
E-mail: order@riverbooksbk.com
www.riverbooksbk.com

Editor: Narisa Chakrabongse
Production supervision: Paisarn Piemmettawat
Design and back cover: Ruetairat Nanta
Cover: Nakrob Moonmanas

ISBN 978 616 451 042 5

Printed and bound in Thailand by Bangkok Printing Co., Ltd.

Contents

Acknowledgements

The writing of this story could not have happened without the unfailing support and love of my parents; I am grateful to my mother for the family narrative, and my father for the historical insights. We shared so many moments of joy and sorrow at the evocation of these memories of the past. I wish to express my love and gratitude and dedicate this book to them.

Apart from the biographical story, we hope that this memoir will also serve as a testimony which can illuminate a little-known part of history and culture for a younger generation of Lao around the world. It will also be a window into the older traditions of Luang Prabang for many who are discovering this ancient capital in this century.

I would like to express my gratitude to my godmother Susan Wilcox without whom this book would probably have not been written.

Our unfolding conversations, and her enthusiasm and encouragement, gave me the energy and inspiration to recall and bring together the family memories and material about my grandmother. I am also indebted to her for polishing my English.

I would also like to thank members of my family who have been helpful in providing photographs and archives.

I would like to express my gratitude to Robyn Lyons, who kindly gave suggestion and sound advice.

With Dayaneetha De Silva I enjoyed many insights and benefited greatly from her experience of the publishing world.

I especially thank her for being the link between Mom Rajawongse Narisa Chakrabongse and myself. I could not have hoped for a better interlocutor for the publishing of this book, with her deep knowledge of traditional cultures in Southeast Asia.

Foreword

The transcription in Lao language of the terms mentioned is indicated in the footnotes. All Lao terms are transcribed according to the traditional pronunciation of Luang Prabang and the Lao script used at the time of the narrative.

Government of the Kingdom of Luang Prabang

At the end of the eighteenth century, under Siamese influence, the government of the Kingdom of Luang Prabang was composed of four bodies: the Great Lineage or 'Great Palace' *(Vang Luang[1])* invested with supreme power; the Front Lineage or 'Front Palace' *(Vang Na[2])*, reporting to the Viceroy, Marshal of the Armies; the Rear Lineage or 'Rear Palace' *(Vang Lang[3])*, in charge of Supply; and the Middle Lineage or 'Middle Palace' *(Vang Kang[4])*, Head of Finance.

From the reign of Manthathourath (1818-1836), under Siamese pressure, the hereditary function of viceroy *(Ouparat[5])* in charge of Military affairs for the Kingdom of Luang Prabang was assigned to the Front House, in order to compete with the king's power.

At that time, under the governance of the four Houses, the administration consisted of many departments *(kom[6])*, including:

> - *kom pravang[7]*, in charge of the affairs of the Royal Palace;
> - *komma khoun[8]*, in charge of the Royal treasury;
> - *kom mahadlek[9]*, in charge of the guard of the Royal Palace;
> - *komma sang[10]*, in charge of the Royal stores, provisions and weapons;
> - *komma na[11]*, in charge of the Royal rice fields;
> - *kom phama[12]*, in charge of the Royal horses;
> - *komma sang[13]*, in charge of the Royal elephants;

> *kom siphay*[14], in charge of the Royal barges;
> *kom phamo*[15], in charge of the Royal health.

Titulature

The titles granted by the king to the higher officers of the army and administration include, in ascending order, the following grades:

1. *phya*[16], followed by the name in relation to the position of the person concerned;
2. *phanya*[17], followed by a term with spatial connotations such as *na neua*[18] ('rice field of Upstream'), *na taeuy*[19] ('rice field of Downstream'), *muang khoua*[20] ('city of Right'), *muang say*[21] ('city of Left'), *muang kang*[22] ('city of Middle'), or as a symbolic reference to the number of men subject to the authority of the holder such as *mun na*[23] ('ten thousand faces');
3. *tiao phanya*[24], followed by one of the preceding names, eg *tiao phanya muang khoua*[25] ('tiao phanya of the city of Right');
4. *tiao phanya luang*[26], composed of *tiao phanya* and *luang* ('great'), denotes the highest rank of the Lao military- administrative hierarchy. It is followed by the name of a large city of strategic importance. There were three *tiao phanya luang*, in descending order:

> *tiao phanya luang muang saen*[27];
> *tiao phanya luang muang chan*[28];
> *tiao phanya luang muang phaen*[29].

These titles probably date back to the 14th century, the time of Fa Ngum, the unifier of the Kingdom of the Million Elephants.

The term *tiao*[30], preceding the above mentioned titles, is a particle indicating nobility. Nevertheless, as a result of their achievements, some commoners could obtain one of the titles in question, including the particle. On the occasion of national ceremonies the holders of these titles paraded on the backs of royal elephants like the great princes. Their descendants formed an intermediate class, of high status, close to the high nobility with which they frequently maintained matrimonial ties. In this narrative we shall call it the 'aristocracy'.

The term 'commoner' will apply to the whole non-titled population.

The following are the titles of territorial administrators, in descending order:

1. *tiao khouaeng*[31] (or *nay khouaeng*[32]), governor of province;
2. *tiao muang*[33], originally designated the lord of a principality but came to be applied to a mayor or district chief;
3. *nay kong*[34], chief of a sub-district;
4. *tassaeng*[35], chief of a township;
5. *nay ban*[36], village chief.

Moreover, the king could grant honorific titles to persons who did not belong to the administration but who distinguished themselves by meritorious deeds.

Appellations

Until the 1940s, the most common names in Luang Prabang were *Kaeo, Khoun, Chan, Saeng, Sing, Souk, Sao, Sy, Daeng, Dam, Di, Douang, Ta, Tan, Tu, Toun, Thi, Bou, Boua, Pane, Pin, Peng, Pong, Phan, Phao, Phaeng, Pheng, Pheuy, Phay, Phoui, Phiou, Phou, Fan, Fong, Mao, Man, Mi, Lek, La, Ouane, On, Oun, Vaen*[37]. There were no surnames and people were known by their ancestry or their district or village of origin. Like the members of the nobility, to distinguish the members of the aristocracy from the common people, the prefixes *kham*[38] or *thong*[39] ('gold') were added to the given name of anyone whose father had the title *phya* or *phanya*.

Under Siamese influence, this practice was abandoned by the members of the Front Lineage, and some of the Great Lineage, in favour of names of Sanskrit or Pali origin. Because of the confusion that all these *kham* prefixes created among Luang Prabang families, the aristocracy also adopted new names.

➤ The term *tiao* is specific to noble men and women;
➤ The term *thao*[40] is specific to noble and aristocratic men;

- The term *nang*[41] is specific to women of the nobility and of the aristocracy;
- The term *nang phya*[42] designates the wife of an aristocrat, whether her husband is titled *phya* or *phanya*;
- In Luang Prabang tradition, the term *houa*[43] is used more often in speech. Literally it means the 'head' which is the most sacred part of the body. Therefore this term is used to emphasise the aristocratic origin of the person in question and means 'the honourable';
- The term *mom*[44] designates an aristocratic or common-law woman married to a nobleman;
- The term *sathou*[45] either designates the abbot of a temple or a prince of high rank;
- The term *sathou nying*[46] designates a princess of high rank;
- The term *tiao mom*[47] designates the first grade of monkhood before becoming *sathou;*
- The term *chan*[48] (diminutive of *achan*[49]) refers to an man who has returned to secular life after a period of ordination in adulthood during which he spent at least several Buddhist lents as monk (*phra*[50]).
- The term *thid*[51] refers to a man who has returned to secular life after a short period of ordination in adulthood.
- The term *xieng*[52] refers to a child who has returned to secular life after a period of ordination in childhood as *joua*[53] (novice).
- The term *bao*[54] means 'man' and is opposed to *sao*[55], 'girl', both of common origin. The *bao* was in this capacity corvéable by the royal administration, but exempt from any chore if he were assigned to the service of a high official.

Prologue

When History and Karma intertwine

In the seventeenth century King Souriya Vongsa restored to the Lan Sang Hom Khao (Kingdom of the Million Elephants and White Parasol), whose capital had been established in Vientiane the previous century, the greatness it had known in the time of his ancestor Fa Ngum, the country's unifier in the fourteenth century.

Its territories extended widely on both banks of the Mekong River, from the Chinese border of Yunnan in the north to the Khong Falls, bordering Cambodia to the south.

King Souriya Vongsa's reign was marked by a great cultural and spiritual development, and the application of law to all classes. The law condemned to death anyone seducing another man's wife. When the king's only son seduced the wife of a high court official, he rendered himself liable to the same penalty and was put to death. Thus the king was deprived of a direct heir.

On the king's death in 1694, his grandsons were too young to assume the throne and fled to Luang Prabang, in the north while the throne was taken in succession by his Prime Minister and son-in-law, then by the viceroy of the southern territories residing at Nakhon on the right bank of the Mekong. From the beginning of the eighteenth century the Lan Sang Hom Khao was thus split into two entities, the Kingdom of Luang Prabang in the north, and the Kingdom of Vientiane in the centre and south. The latter split in turn in 1713 to form the Kingdom of Champassak.

In 1752, incited by the Kingdom of Vientiane, the Burmese Kingdom of Ava invaded and subjugated Luang Prabang, deporting six hundred hostages, among them the king's brother. As the Burmese threat persisted, Siam entered into an alliance with Luang Prabang in 1776 against Ava, marking the start of Siamese influence in Luang Prabang.

In 1792, fleeing the attack of the Vientiane troops, Anourouth, the King of Luang Prabang took refuge with Phra Buddha Yodfa Chulalok, the King of Siam[1], entrusting the regency of the kingdom during four years to his young Prime Minister Tiao Phanya Luang Muang Saen[2], also known as Tiao Phanya Luang Muang Saen Khaeo Khao ('Great-Lord-with-White-Teeth'[3]), in reference to the colour of his teeth.

According to the administrative organisation of the time, the prime minister exercised not only a political function, but also those of the Commander-in-Chief of the Army *(ok thab ok seuk[4])* and the Governor of the capital. Because of this, he was the most important personage in the kingdom after the monarch.

Unlike the royal residence which was located on the upstream area of Luang Prabang, the prime minister's residence was located in the downstream area, close to Vat That temple, and was hence known as the 'Downstream Mansion' *(hong taeuy[5])*. According to the expression sanctioned by use, the prime minister 'ate half the city' *(kin thong muang[6])*, his position conferring him the homage of his vassals and the right to collect tributes[7]. Indeed, his stronghold extended from Vat Houa Xieng[8] and Vat That[9] quarters to the outskirts of Tao Mou[10], and included Nong Samouth[11] (now renamed Nong Kham[12]), a lake which he had dug by his slaves and which was big enough to host solemn pirogue races every year on the ninth lunar month (July-August), Sieng Kaeo[13], Ban Khay[14] and Ban Khoy[15].

On the withdrawal of the Vientiane army, contrary to all expectations, Anourouth was placed under house arrest in Bangkok. Tiao Phanya Luang Muang Saen had to send two emissaries to the Court of China to expose the abnormal situation to the emperor himself and obtain his help for the release of his king in 1796.

On the latter's death in 1818 his son Manthathourath ascended the throne of Luang Prabang under the aegis of Siam. In order to circumscribe the powers of Tiao Phanya Luang Muang Saen, a dynasty of viceroys, named 'Vang Na' (Front Palace), in charge of military affairs, was established on the Siamese model[16]. Prince Oun Kaeo was its first beneficiary in 1820. Tiao Phanya Luang Muang Saen, deprived of his high office, had been entrusted with dangerous operations on the front of the battles. In 1839, he was killed 'on the neck of his elephant'.

On the night after the news of his death reached Luang Prabang, a body of armed commandos looted his home, the Downstream Mansion and ruthlessly expelled its inhabitants, including his three granddaughters, Thong-Sy, Kham-Tu and Kham-Phiou, whom he had raised since they became orphaned at an early age. Their outcries and tears were quickly stifled by the threat of arms. In a few minutes the incident was closed. Vang Na's family settled there. The victims, totally deprived of their possessions, took refuge with relatives in the near neighbourhood. Such was the fear inspired by this ruthless act that for almost a century no one dared speak the name of the former Prime Minister[17].

Nevertheless from that time onwards, the collective memory of the family was nourished by the recurring reminder of events: to each generation passing before the Downstream Mansion, the descendants of Tiao Phanya Luang Muang Saen whispered in their children's ear: 'Look, this is where our ancestor lived!'

It is against the background of these long past events that our story begins, testimony to destinies in which tradition, family rivalries and karma intermingle. This is the story of my grandmother, Mom Kham-Phiou and of the particular connection linking her at all the stages of her life to the Downstream Mansion.

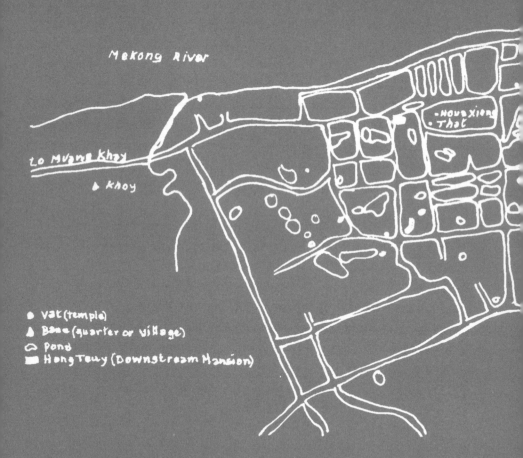

Mekong River

Lo Muong Khay

▲ khay

- Houaxieng
  · That

● Vat (temple)
▲ Bane (quarter or village)
⌒ Pond
■ HongThuy (Downstream Mansion)

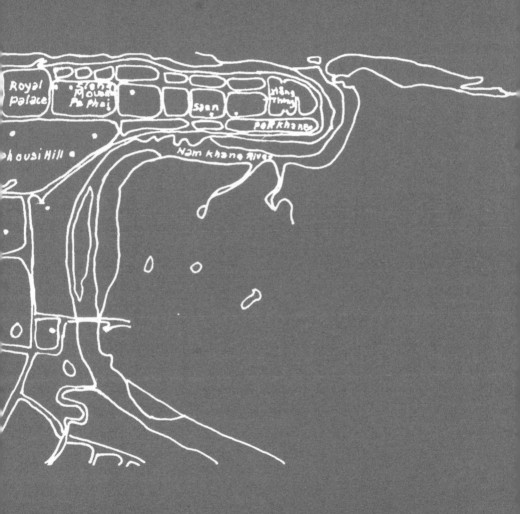

Chapter 1

The Pimay festivities in 1930

L et us now return to the year 1930 and the celebrations of Pimay (New Year) in that year of the Horse in Luang Prabang, the ancient royal capital of Laos, a still largely feudal city with clear distinctions between classes and rigid rules of etiquette covering almost every aspect of behaviour.

Pimay is the principal annual festival, the three days marking the passing of the old year and the beginning of the new. The first day, corresponding to the last day of the past year, includes three tasks: the general cleaning of the house; the shopping in the great market full of plants, flowers and every sort of vegetable but especially during the morning, of small living animals, birds, tortoises, fishes, eels which the purchasers will set free in the afternoon; and the descent of the Buddha statues from the altars in houses and temples[1] in order to be showered with scented water by the population.

All these actions are aimed at expelling the bad things of the previous year and gaining spiritual merits for the new one ahead.

The second day represents the gap between the old and new year: for some it is a day of rest, for others it is a day for entertainment, in particular for the procession of monks led by the abbots in their palanquins from Vat That temple, located downstream of the city, to Vat Xieng Thong temple located upstream. All along the procession route the monks are showered with scented water *(nam song phra[2])* by the bystanders.

The monks are followed by rows of young girls with their parasols,

The market in Luang Prabang in the 1930s.

musicians, dancers, and men wearing masks of the Pou Gneu Gna Gneu[3], accompanied by their lion puppet from the Himalayas, Sing Kaeo Sing Kab[4]. The last group in the procession is composed of men in ludicrous clothes, representing bad things. They are copiously showered with muddy water.

Once they arrive at Vat Xieng Thong, the monks of Vat That shower the Buddha statues there with water scented with seasonal flowers, leaves or fruit pods that have been dried such as *dok kham[5]*, *dok kham phama[6]*, *dok no[7]*, *dok nom ngoua[8]*, *dok sone[9]*, *dok khai nao[10]*, *dok i houb[11]*, *dok say heun[12]*, *dok tang[13]*, *van phai[14]*, and *som poy[15]*.

Not only did the Pimay ceremonies celebrate the annual passage of the year but also the supremacy of women over men. This playful inversion of the norm was fully expressed in the afternoon when the population moved to the long beach, Done Say Muang Khoun, on the opposite bank of the Mekong to build sand pyramids decorated with zodiacal banners as a tribute to the celestial and aquatic divinities.

It was at this moment that hordes of women rushed upon the men, blackening their faces with soot, ripping their shirts to pieces and throwing them unceremoniously into the river. Men had no right to defend themselves. Their only salvation was the speed of their legs!

The whole population participated in these festivties, with the exception of women from the nobility and the aristocracy, for whom joining in this kind of demonstration was not appropriate, for in the Lao society of the time, it was inconceivable that a woman belonging to the aristocracy would sing, dance or play music.

The third day is New Year's day. During the alms giving on this particular day, the monks receive offerings in abundance such as rice, cakes, money, and fruits. All of these gifts were aimed at obtaining future well-being.

In the afternoon, the procession took the opposite direction, from the upstream temple to the downstream temple, and the monks of Vat Xieng Thong showered the Buddha statues of Vat That Luang with scented water.

From New Year's day on, and over a few ensuing days people would perform a ritual of homage to their parents and older relatives in different areas of Luang Prabang. The ritual, named *soma*[16], consisted of an offering made in a silver cup *(o[17])* for women or in a silver stem cup *(khan[18])* for men, of a cone of banana leaves *(van[19])* filled with flowers and a pair of wax candles[20]. Apart from the sacred aspect of the ritual, it was also a way of reaffirming and consolidating complex family ties over several generations.

On the morning of the first day of the festival, all along the main road, people would try to outdo each other with beautiful costumes in shining colours: the men wearing many coloured *sampots* with a white shirt or vest, the young girls in silk scarves and skirts garlanded with flowers and adorned with golden jewels – chains with a golden flower bud on top around their chignons, golden necklaces around their necks, bracelets on their wrists, golden earrings in their ears and antique rings with precious stones on their fingers. It was an occasion to show off family jewels and wealth.

Nang Kham-Phiou at 16.

As the young girls walked along their anklets clinked, the solid silver making a clear ringing sound while the lighter, hollow silver ones merely emitting a dull clunk. The sounds also indicated the status and wealth of the girl's family as well the single status of young unmarried girls.

Girls were strictly chaperoned, with young men and girls prohibited from meeting each other, so that for the young men the main interest of the festival was the chance to at least look at girls. With this in mind, they paraded up and down in front of the stalls where the pretty girls were gathered.

The purpose of the stalls, either side of the main road, was not to make money but to give an opportunity for the girls selling small items such as candles, flowers, cigarettes to see and be seen by young men. They still could not speak to one another but could at least look and

Nang Kham-Phiou and a neighbour.

perhaps even exchange glances under the watchful eyes of the chaperone.

Any further contact would then be up to the families to decide: any courtship, under the close surveillance of sisters, aunts and chaperones, and eventual marriages were settled only by parents.

On this first day of Pimay in 1930, a group of older noblemen – both married and bachelors – in their best attire were also promenading. They wandered at ease from stall to stall enjoying the displays. People were delighted at their taking part in the festival.

Soon the group paused in front of the stall where Nang Kham-Phiou was with her chaperone and friends. She was a slim girl, her skin the colour of mother of pearl. She wore little or no makeup and, her long wavy black hair was coiled into a bun with a short fringe of curly hair in front.

Her huge luminous eyes were already causing havoc: several families with eligible sons were making preliminary approaches to her mother regarding marriage.

On that day, like other young girls, she was adorned with jewels, and wore a lilac-coloured silk blouse, a dark red skirt decorated with silver thread and a scarf of the same colour. She was shaded by a little umbrella of pink silk with a chiseled silver handle, with a golden lacquered basket *(sa nam kiaeng[21])* hanging on her arm.

Standing in full view and outshining her circle of friends, she attracted general admiration. She recognised most of the members of the group of noblemen except for one, an adult who, dazzled by her beauty, stared fixedly at her. On her side she made a mental note of him – his dull red *sampot*, his beige coat, his trilby, and the camera on his shoulder. She saw a handsome, well-dressed man. Intrigued and surprised by the attention she was paying to his appearance, she whispered to her friend sitting next to her:

"Who is he?"

"Don't you know? He is Prince Souvanna Phouma[22]. He has just come back from France – he is an engineer," whispered her better informed neighbour, proud of her knowledge.

Kham-Phiou herself had never heard of him or even known of his existence. At the same time, he was making discreet enquiries, speaking in French, about her from his brother-in-law, Prince Souvannarath[23]. The latter explained: "She is the most courted girl in Luang Prabang, the daughter of the late Tiao Phanya Luang Mun Na[24]."

Meanwhile the group's prolonged stay at the stall was attracting astonished attention.

Suddenly, Prince Souvanna Phouma addressed Kham-Phiou directly, asking for locally-made hand-rolled cigarettes. His bold stare and direct request to an unmarried girl outraged

Sa nam kiaeng.

all local custom. An embarrassed Kham-Phiou blushed, kept her eyes lowered and made no answer, well aware that the rules of protocol forbade her speaking directly to an older person of higher rank.

Her nanny *(mae nom[25])* swiftly came to her aid, embarrassedly explaining to the group that the stall did not belong to Kham-Phiou but to her friend. At these words, Souvanna Phouma took advantage to address Kham-Phiou:

"You could well help your friend prepare a parcel for me!"

Kham-Phiou's cheeks ever grew ever more scarlet from emotion and shyness. Keeping her eyes lowered, she felt paralysed and unable to make any move. At last, at the insistence of her friend Onesy[26] she managed to wrap the cigarettes in a banana leaf and placed it on the counter for the buyer to pick up. He still vainly insisted that she handed it to him personally. The little play had lasted some half an hour much to the amused astonishment of the group and those around them.

Later Souvanna Phouma himself admitted that her modest behaviour had both delighted and moved him, recalling to him memories of his childhood in Luang Prabang, which he had missed so deeply during his long years of absence in France.

At this period in Luang Prabang, direct courtship was not permitted and lovers had to make do with remote flirtation through the eyes. Only on the long-awaited marriage day would they have real contact.

The final day before the Pimay festival is filled with promises and changes: the rituals of cleansing the house, dusting, sweeping and generally cleaning, getting rid of old or unwanted things and then decorating the house with flowers.

It is on this day too that the animals that have been bought are freed when the drums signal the removal of the statues of the Buddha from their altars to be washed with scented water, both at home and in the temples. And finally, at the end of the day when everything is accomplished people go to the Mekong River to wash their hair with water that had been used to soak sticky rice the day before *(nam mouak[27])* and into which kaffir lime had been squeezed *(mak khi houd[28])*. All this is part of the day's traditional activities.

Prince Souvanna Phouma was restless, and unable to remain still. He wanted to visit the house of the young girl whom he had seen earlier in the morning. To give the visit a veneer of respectability, he persuaded his brother-in-law to accompany him on the excuse of passing on news of Kham-Phiou's elder brother Kham-Phay, who was studying medicine in Hanoi. Any excuse will serve when one has fallen head over heels in love and where, as here, the excuse can be a delicate compliment displaying interest and respect for the family concerned.

Conversation at Kham-Phiou's home, hampered both by the embarrassment of the visitors and by the hostess's mistrust, faltered with the real reason for the visit remaining unspoken. Kham-Phiou's mother was unforthcoming, being totally opposed to a marriage alliance with any member of the noble families.

Kham-Phiou herself was away with all her friends bathing and washing their hair in the Mekong River, just down in the Sieng Mouane Quarter, facing Phou Thao-Phou Nang, two hills located on the opposite bank. These hills are known in the legendary landscape of Luang Prabang for having been the theatre of a tragic and eternal love story. A Cambodian queen named Nanta, described in this context as an ogress *(nyakkhini)*[29], ordered her daughter Nang Kanghi to seduce the prince of Luang Prabang. Contrary to her mother's plan, Nang Kanghi instead fell in love with the prince, and in order to win him, chased him in a desperate pursuit. At the end of the ordeal, the exhausted protagonists, collapsed and died, the head of one on the feet of the other. Their bodies were transformed into two hills: 'the mountain of the prince and the mountain of the princess' (Phou Thao-Phou Nang)[30].

Kham-Phiou was coming up the river bank when she was startled to see the prince coming towards her and complaining that she had spent so much time in the river. Deeply embarrassed and blushing, while very conscious that her wet clothes were clinging to her body, she could not think of a reply.

His actions were another offence to tradition, for it was not proper for a man openly to look at a woman while she was taking her bath.

If it were someone else, the village headman would certainly have intervened and the offender would have had to pay a fine. But it was Souvanna Phouma, a young prince freshly graduated from France and no one dared to say anything.

Kham-Phiou attempted to hurry past him without speaking, but she was hampered by her clothes. Heavy and sodden with water they stuck to her legs so that she was unable to move at all quickly. Having been brought up to be physically modest, she was overcome with embarrassment at having only a bathing dress covering her breasts and legs and a towel about her shoulders with her long wet hair clinging to her back.

The prince himself was both amused and satisfied with the effect he had produced and also delighted that she continued the tradition of a daily bathe at sunset. He took advantage of the meeting to ask her if she did not want to hear news of her elder brother, but could get no answer.

Indeed, at this first meeting alone together he could only get an occasional faint "yes" or "no" from the embarrassed Kham-Phiou.

Chapter 2

Towards marriage

From the moment Souvanna Phouma had seen Kham-Phiou at the great market he had fallen deeply in love and now devoted all his efforts to courtship. Kham-Phiou sat, as custom dictated, on the veranda of her mother's house, always chaperoned by either her mother or Mae Pheng, her old nanny, sitting not far behind her.

Every evening Souvanna Phouma accompanied by his page Bao Chan carrying an oil lamp, walked the three kilometres to and from her house.

Kham-Phiou herself scarcely spoke, restricting her answers to a "yes" or "no". From time to time the *mae nom* tried to help by answering for her but was invariably snubbed by the prince with the words:

"I am talking to Kham-Phiou," which made Kham-Phiou secretly rejoice at her nanny's speechless expression.

Souvanna Phouma was strong, self assured and of royal birth, a superior being in Luang Prabang society. His passion did not lessen, and he was determined to marry Kham-Phiou. After only a week, an intermediary *(mae su[1])* was sent to open negotiations prior to a marriage proposal.

Against every expectation, Nang Phya Kham-Douang returned a negative but polite answer. She said:

"My daughter is too young, she is not adult enough for marriage and does not even know how to cook. Please ask His Highness to forgive us."[2]

The wording of her answer was code for pointing out that Souvanna Phouma, in his thirties, was according to Lao custom, far too old to be considered a suitable husband for a girl of 16. The prince who had lived abroad for the last twenty years either missed the point or deliberately chose not to understand it.

Souvanna Phouma was not willing to give up, coming in person to assure his intended future mother-in-law that Kham-Phiou would not be expected to cook or manage a household – he had staff to do all that.

Their evening meetings in front of witnesses continued. The prince urged his hoped for fiancée to make a decision herself. But Kham-Phiou would only say: "It is for my mother to decide"[3], the proper submission to parental wishes dictated by her upbringing.

She had grown up in a family environment from which coarseness and vulgarity were excluded both in language and attitudes. Language was very codified and depended both on circumstances and to whom one was speaking. If she was addressing her parents, monks, any member of the nobility or aristocracy older than herself then she would term herself 'khanoy'[4] (your little subject) and address the monks or nobles as 'thou'[5] and the aristocrats as 'houa'[6] (the honourable).

When addressing a person of the same rank as herself, she spoke of herself as 'khoy'[7] (I), and the other person as 'tiao'[8] (you).

By contrast when addressing a person of inferior rank, the tradition in Luang Phrabang was for a master to speak of himself as 'o'[9] and address the servant as 'to'[10].

Despite his lack of progress, Souvanna Phouma continued to urge Kham-Phiou, pressing his half brother and brother-in-law to support him but not to avail.

The prince was not the first to seek Nang Phya Kham-Douang daughter's hand in marriage. There had been approaches through intermediaries from several respected families with young hopefuls, but she considered her daughter too young for marriage and had politely discouraged the advances. In those cases the problem was not the difference in age as with Souvanna Phouma, but the age of Kham-Phiou herself whom Nang Phya Kham-Douang considered still too young and immature for marriage.

At that time religious festivals were an opportunity for the young people to meet and the traditional court of love was held in the grounds of the temple. The young men, sometimes covering their faces with a scarf so as not to be recognised, were seated in line opposite the women. Then, accompanied by a traditional orchestra composed of a xylophone *(lanat)[11]*, a drum *(kong[12])*, two kinds of violas *(so i[13], so ou[14])* and a pair of small bells *(sing[15])*, and sometimes a cithar *(khim[16])*, or more simply by the traditional mouth organ *(khaen[17])*, the two groups competed with alternate songs and showed their talent, with the help of experienced older men and women who whispered answers. The principal repertoires were *'Khap thoum'[18]*, *'Salang sam sao'[19]* and *'An nang su'[20]*, whose themes could be standard or improvised. The jousts, accompanied by the traditional rice alcohol *(lao lao[21])* , ended late in the night, with laughter and verbal provocations full of wit which at times could be saucy on both sides. All this of course was not at all acceptable for the women of the aristocracy. It was notorious that one of them, from the neighbourhood of Ban Sieng Mouane, with a particularly lively and intelligent character, had been able to resist replying with a great deal of skill to a suitor who tickled her, causing a stir in the whole neighbourhood. Later, it transpired that the young person in question had secretly learned all the repartees of the traditional jousts. And although she was the eldest daughter of an important person, no eligible man from an aristocratic family in Luang Prabang would venture to marry her!

Apart from these occasions, at other times the young man could go to the veranda of the house of his beloved to flirt. One day a young prince of the Great Lineage, his head and face covered with a light scarf, came to Kham-Phiou's, and, adopting a country accent, asked: "Young girl, give me some water, please..." In Lao houses it was customary to have at the entrance of the house a terracotta jar filled with fresh and clean water for the use of passers-by. Kham-Phiou, who had recognised her suitor in spite of his disguise, answered him bluntly: 'You can see that the water is there!'

Even the Deputy French Resident, after seeing Kham-Phiou when she accompanied her mother who went to the Residence to draw her pension as the widow of Tiao Phanya Luang Mun Na, made an offer of marriage. This young man, respecting local tradition and custom, sent an emissary to Ban Sieng Mouane stating that he would like to make a proposal for Kham-Phiou's hand in marriage. He stated that he came from a good family, that he undertook to ensure Kham-Phiou learnt French and that he would take her to France to meet his family.

This proposal horrified Nang Phya Kham-Douang who immediately kept her daughter indoors. She only permitted her to go out if well guarded and took all possible precautions before letting her out of the house.

Just as she was opposed to her daughter marrying into Souvanna Phouma's family, it was equally inconceivable that she might marry into a French family however respectable. Fresh in her memory was the fate which had befallen one of her relatives who, ignoring the family ban, married a French planter based in Vietnam and was henceforth an outcast to her family and relations.

The episode of the Deputy Resident's proposal went no further and in future it would be the old nanny who accompanied Nang Phya Kham-Douang on any future visits to the French Residence!

This time, hoping to get rid of the importunate and unwelcome suitor that Souvanna Phouma represented, Kham-Phiou's mother claimed that her daughter was already engaged to a cousin and that a dowry of 100 piastres had been settled.

Unhesitatingly the prince answered that he was prepared to offer a dowry of 200 piastres from which 100 could be used to repay the dowry deposit. This huge sum, far outweighing the dowry even a princess could traditionally expect, stunned Nang Phya Kham-Douang and caused a scandal in the prince's family.

Once the problem of the dowry had been resolved, the prospective mother-in-law immediately raised another argument against the marriage.

"Forgive me," she said to the prince, "but Kham-Phiou is my eldest daughter and is needed for the education of her younger brother and sisters Kham-Pheuy, Kham-Phaeng and Kham-Pin. If she leaves there will only be the old nanny and a young servant in the house. Please understand the very difficult situation of the household since the death of my husband. The change of currency decreed by the French administration[22] has also contributed to the financial difficulties of the family. It will be rendered still more difficult if my daughter leaves."

"Please do not worry over that," replied the prince without hesitation, "I shall make you a monthly allowance of 20 piastres[23] to employ someone to take charge of the younger children."

Silenced by this unforeseen response, his prospective mother-in-law found nothing to say and had no other arguments to bring forward. She could have claimed that Kham-Phiou had no inclination towards the prince but this would have been untrue. On the contrary, the two protagonists saw each other every evening on the veranda at the courting hour, sitting well apart under the vigilant eye of the *mae nom* according to traditional custom, but both hoping with all their hearts that they would soon be granted permission to marry from Nang Phya Kham-Douang.

Nang Phya Kham-Douang with her daughter Kham-Pin.

Nang Phya Kham-Douang with her daughters Kham-Phaeng and Kham-Pin.

Prince Souvannarath returning from an audience at the Royal Palace,
Luang Prabang, 1925.

In fact, the reluctance of Nang Phya Kham-Douang was due to two main reasons. The first related to the place of residence of the bride and groom. Unlike the commoner and aristocratic tradition that the son-in-law lived at his mother-in-law's house (which actually would be of benefit to her), the union with a nobleman meant that she would be living at her parents-in-law's house.

Families that were modest or attracted by social advancement might seek this type of alliance, but for aristocrats wealthy and titled by the king for several generations such a move was seen as disadvantageous. It meant the loss of an active agent in the family unit, especially hard if it was the eldest daughter. Moreover, living with her in-laws, Kham-Phiou's fate would be left to their goodwill.

The second reason was the rank of women. A commoner or an aristocrat, even if she were the first to marry her husband, could be relegated to the position of a secondary wife when her husband took a noble wife.

Despite the sincere love that Prince Souvanna Phouma seemed to express for her daughter, Nang Phya Kham-Douang knew that the latter could potentially be a victim of this scenario.

A recent example had occurred in Luang Prabang when a prince of a collateral branch of the royal family, seduced by the beauty of a young commoner girl named Douang, wanted to marry her. His family opposed it, but he persevered, married his beloved and settled in her home. Shortly afterwards, she became pregnant. The prince's family did not capitulate and strove to find him a noble woman day and night. In the end, the bridegroom admitted defeat and married one of his cousins.

On the day of the ceremony, his first wife, seven months pregnant and in despair, exiled herself to distant relatives in the former Lanna kingdom, in northern Siam[24].

Another case was that of a young girl, also a commoner, married to a prince of the Great Lineage without parental consent. He had taken up residence with his wife's parents but unable to resist the constant pressure of his family, the prince reluctantly agreed to marry a young lady from the Downstream Mansion. His first wife, eight months pregnant at the time, was relegated to concubine status.

Rebellious and unlike in the previous case in which the victim had submitted to her fate, she responded with a lot of courage. On the day of the ceremony, as the procession carrying her substitute to the residence of her future husband was passing, she placed herself on the edge of the street, ostentatiously displaying her belly as a way of telling her that the unborn child would be deprived of a father. Later, when he was of school age, the child was entrusted to his father.

But unhappily, as far as Souvanna Phouma and Kham-Phiou were concerned, days and nights continued in the same way with no progress. The prince, not receiving a response from Nang Phya Kham-Douang, became impatient and exhorted Kham-Phiou to take the decision herself. However whatever were her own feelings, and even if her heart were to break, it was inconceivable to Kham-Phiou that she could act without her mother's consent.

In the face of her refusal, the prince threatened to make use of a right – suggested by an accomplice brother-in-law – to which his noble status entitled him with regard to lesser ones, even well-known ancient aristocratic ones, to simply move into the house of the young girl without the family having the right to object and without any ceremony or question of dowry.

Indochinese piastre.

Not only would this deprive the family in question of material advantages, but it would also represent an immeasurable loss of face in Luang Prabang good society.

Such a prospect could not be entertained by Nang Phya Kham-Douang, and the following day she gave her consent, but on a final condition – that the request for the hand of Kham-Phiou must be made by the family of the prince to her late husband's father, Kham-Pheng, Tiao Phanya Na Neua, considered the family patriarch. Although she had given in, Nang Phya Kham-Douang still required an honourable defeat at the expense of the prince's family.

This demand by a person of lower status than the prince was unheard of and a bombshell to the prince's family. His elder sister, Princess Sa-Ngiem Kham was stunned and was subjected to enormous pressure from her other half brothers, who had been hoping to marry their own daughters to the prince. They exhorted her to categorically refuse the pretentious and scandalous proposal of Nang Phya Kham-Douang.

All these self-interested objections disgusted Souvanna Phouma. Now that all the obstacles from the family of Kham-Phiou had been overcome, it was his own family who were creating problems.

Accordingly, he announced that if he was not allowed to marry Kham-Phiou he would return to France, as she was the one and only person he wished to marry. In the face of such a declaration there was nothing else that his family could do.

Faced with the uproar from Princess Sa-Ngiem Kham's family and the deadlocked situation, Prince Souvannarath, the husband of Princess Sa-Ngiem Kham, took the initiative and went to Tiao Phanya Na Neua to formally ask for the hand of Kham-Phiou for his brother-in-law. Following this interview, the engagement was finalised with the agreed dowry of 200 piastres and a contract allowing 20 piastres a month to the future mother-in-law. A marriage date was duly set.

It is unnecessary to describe the howls and tears of those nieces who saw their hope of marriage with the prince vanish, but it was unclear if they would accept as a fact the forthcoming marriage. One thing that was certain has they had no argument to discredit Kham-Phiou, who was exemplary in her life as a young girl.

Souvanna Phouma later explained to his wife, why there was no question of his agreeing to marry one of his nieces. In the first place, he was not in love with any of them and, secondly, there was the risk regarding the health of children from a marriage with such a close blood relation.

From the beginning of their official engagement, the days and nights seemed to shine more happily on the young couple, enchanted to meet each other every evening. Although the chaperone was still present she sat at a distance and remained silent, leaving them to tease each other, and talk freely.

Souvanna Phouma, who had known a freer life in France admitted he found it hard to comprehend and accept the traditional constraints but nevertheless decided to follow them to the letter.

One evening, whether from curiosity or as a challenge, he could not prevent himself from cornering his fiancée to get the answer he so much desired.

"We shall soon be celebrating our marriage, so now tell me that you too want to marry me."

Kham-Phiou blushed a deep red but made no answer. She felt she would faint; no other young Lao man would have dared to ask such a direct question.

Souvanna Phouma insisted: "Since the first time we saw each other at the market, I have been overcome with love for you... but, if by chance, it is only out of obedience to your grandfather and your mother that you are marrying me, I should be very unhappy and miserable but I could think again. Please answer me honestly."

Blushing even deeper, in a faint childish voice, Kham-Phiou said: "Since this is so, I am willing."[25]

Deeply moved, softened and overcome by this simple shy reply, Souvanna Phouma went home even deeper in love.

Chapter 3

The wedding

Following Luang Prabang traditions, a wedding, in order to ensure the success of the marriage, must be arranged according to strict protocol regarding the time and date based on the lunar calendar and the zodiac of that year. Furthermore, custom reserved odd months, in particular the ninth lunar month, for nobles, while commoners could only marry in even ones.

To complicate the issue even more there were the three Lenten months in the Buddhist calendar, the seventh, eighth and ninth months[1] during which no marriages could be celebrated.

As Souvanna Phouma did not want to postpone the wedding to the tenth lunar month, it was necessary to arrange it before the end of the sixth lunar month. Given the short period available, despite repeated attempts the astrologers could only find one possible day, the thirteenth day of the rising moon of the sixth lunar month, and even this was not as excellent as would have been desirable but merely passably auspicions.

Souvanna Phouma, fresh from his engineering studies in France, attributed little importance to astrological predictions and announced that passable would suffice. What was important in his eyes was to fix a date for the wedding and not to wait for three months.

In contrast to Souvanna Phouma's casual approach, the selection of a merely 'passable' day shocked the family of Nang Phya Kham-Douang. They would have far preferred a postponement, more particularly as this year, the year of the Horse, like that of the Tiger, was not favourable for marriage. However to avoid further tension and ill feeling they reluctantly raised no objection. After hasty preparations, the wedding was celebrated just a week after the engagement, which was absolutely abnormal and against traditional protocol.

Other formal rules relating to marriage attached particular significance to whether the procession started from the bride or bridegroom's house, the place where the ceremony was held and the future domicile of the couple. These depended on their respective social class and rank. In those days, young couples did not live in a separate household but as part of either the bride or bridegroom's household.

There were four basic categories in Luang Prabang marriage traditions. The first, called 'procession of the son-in-law to the bride's house'[2], related to marriage of men and women of equal rank in the commoner and aristocratic classes. In this case, the bride was implicitly placed in a superior position, as the procession went from the bridegroom's house to that of his future mother-in-law where the marriage was celebrated. Not only did the bridegroom go to his mother-in-law's house for the marriage, he normally lived there afterwards and his mother-in-law remained the head of the household. So far as the bride was concerned, marriage did not change her way of life fundamentally: she remained at home.

But when a woman was of common origin and married an aristocrat or when she was of noble or aristocratic origin and married a man of noble origin, as was the case of Nang Kham-Phiou and Prince Souvanna Phouma, the position of the man undoubtedly predominated over the woman. This system, labelled 'the procession of the daughter-in-law to the palace'[3], was in the bridegroom's favour and it was to his family home the bride came and his family who held the power.

The third type of marriage was called a 'procession on both sides'[4] and involved the union of a man and a woman of equal rank from the nobility[5]. The bridegroom was led to the house of the bride where a short ceremony took place and he then returned home to await his fiancée, who in turn, was led there in procession for an official marriage and to take up formal residence.

A fourth, less formal ceremony, was called 'short recalling of the souls'[6], or 'recalling of the souls over the betel kit'[7]. Here, a simple tray holding ordinary objects including betel leaves which both chewed was used to call the souls. This rite was open to everyone regardless of class or rank. It was used by both rich and poor alike when the marriage was without parental approval. As its name implied, the marriage required only a simple betel set on an undecorated tray. The master of ceremonies was a third person who proceeded to recall the souls of the newlyweds and then united them by tying their wrists together with cotton strings[8].

This minimalist ceremony was also used by kings and princes to acquire a concubine. In such cases the king or prince was not physically present at the ceremony: his presence was symbolised by a jacket belonging to him laid over his tray. In fact, his principal spouse was in charge of the ceremony and the number of guests was limited to the nearest family, with no rejoicing nor meal.

In the early afternoon of the thirteenth day of the waxing moon of the sixth lunar month of the Horse year, corresponding to Saturday 10 May 1930, before leaving the family home, Kham-Phiou performed a *soma* to her mother. In fact, due to her widowhood, and to ward off the risk of negative influences, Nang Phya Kham-Douang did not participate in the procession or the wedding ceremony.

Crouching in front of her mother, Kham-Phiou raised a silver cup *(o)* towards her, bowing her head, while remembering the care she was indebted to her mother for since her birth, and asking pardon for all the faults committed against her. Nang Phya Kham-Douang, seated on a cushion, holding the edge of the *o* as a sign of assent, responded with a long and beautiful formulation ending with the remission of the faults. Then, as Kham-Phiou brought the end of her mother's scarf to her forehead and prostrated at her feet, the latter gently patted her neck with the end of her scarf, saying, 'My daughter, you are forgiven.'

After this emotional interlude, the procession set off. In front walked the male members of the bride's family, bearing the different elements of the 'tray of the bride's souls'[9]. Upon arrival at the home of the future spouse, these elements had to be assembled.

According to Luang Prabang tradition, the structure of the tray of the souls *(pha khouan[10])* is formed by the superimposition of the following three elements, from top to bottom: a silver cup *(o)* lodged within a silver stem cup[11] *(khan)*, which rests on a round lacquered wooden tray *(pha[12])* covered with fresh banana leaves, placed on the floor, on a square of white cotton fabric.

At the upper level, in the middle of the *o*, filled three quarters full with raw sticky rice, is placed a bottle of rice alcohol, wrapped in long white cotton thread[13]. Around it stand six cones in banana leaves filled with a pair of wax candles, fresh flowers and leaves such as *dok horn kai[14]* (plumed cockscomb), *dok dao heuang[15]* (marigold), *baeuy kham baeuy khoun[16]* (croton), *baeuy ngeun baeuy kham[17]* (croton), *baeuy dok hak[18]* (crown flower leaves). The *o* also holds a big wax candle, cones in banana leaves filled with betel leaves[19] *(van phou[20])*, several pairs of skewers of flowers and leaves of *dok hak[21]* (crown flower), *mak jab[22]* (water chestnut) and slices of betel nut.

All these items have auspicious symbolisms for the marriage and are meant to bring happiness and prosperity to the new couple.

Traditional silk and gold embroidered scarves of Luang Prabang.

For example, *dok hak* ('love flower') ensures the love of the couple, *baeuy ngeun baeuy kham* ('silver and gold leaves') their wealth, *mak jab* ('holding fruit') the strong bond of their union.

At the median level, on the tray and around the foot of the *khan* are arranged several elements with auspicious symbolism to attract the souls of the bride: a pair of rhinoceros horns *(no haed[23])*, elephant tusk *(nga sang[24])*, deer horn or boar tusk embellished with a *repoussé* silver base, as well as tools for making the betel quid: a pair of knives with ivory, silver or gold handles *(mid dam nga dam ngeun[25])*, a knife with an ivory or silver handle to peel the bark of the betel nut *(mid pad mak[26])* and the betel nut cracker *(mid sanak[27])*. In addition there were two boiled eggs, a hand of 'egg' bananas *(kouay khai neung vi[28])*, traditional sweetmeats of all kinds *(khao nom khong tone[29])* such as *khao tom[30]* (a cake made of banana, sticky rice and coconut wrapped into banana leaves and steamed), *khao khob[31]* (crispy rice cakes), *khao khi nou[32]* (a sweet made of fried rice flour caramelised with treacle) and *khaonom san[33]* (a cake made of steamed rice flour with several colours and layers).

Traditional silk and silver embroidered skirts of Luang Prabang.

On the lower level, around the foot of the tray are placed a basket of sticky rice *(aeb khao niaeo[34])* and a silver betel set *(khan mak[35])*. A silver ewer *(nam tao ngeun[36])* completes the ritual items.

The struggle between the two families had been followed avidly by the Luangprabangese. News of the unusual outcome of discussions for the wedding day attracted general curiosity and led to a large crowd following the bridal procession. The procession took 1.5 kilometres to wend its way from the maternal house of Kham-Phiou in Sieng Mouane Quarter to the Downstream Mansion *(Hong Taeuy)* in Vat That Quarter. The mansion had been occupied since 1820 by the line of the Viceroy *(Vang Na)*. It was there that Princess Sa-Ngiem Kham was waiting for the young couple who were to live with her.

Protected from the sun by an umbrella carried by a woman at her side, Kham-Phiou surrounded by her close female relatives followed after the male relatives and at the tail of the procession came other family members, friends, and neighbours, men and women walking together.

Kham-Phiou wore a double-breasted jacket *(seua pay[37])* and a skirt *(sin[38])* made of aubergine-coloured brocade – a fabric traditionally imported from China and a colour reserved for members of the aristocracy – with her favourite purple scarf *(pha biaeng[39])* woven and embroidered with designs in gold thread. The carefully chosen colours complemented each other and accentuated her unusually white skin. Her long dark curly hair had been skilfully arranged into a bun around which a gold chain *(say khong[40])* and a chain of gold beads *(mak toum[41])* were wound, fixed and surmounted by diverse gold hairpins *(pak phom[42], dok vai[43])*.

Her natural beauty and becoming outfit were further enhanced by family gold jewels: long spherical earrings *(tang[44])*, necklaces *(say kho[45])* and many gold bead chains *(mak toum)* around her neck, plain bracelets *(pok khaen kiaeng[46])*, different kinds of twisted bracelets *(pok khaen fan[47], pok khaen katoy[48])* on her arms, sapphire rings on her fingers and a ringed belt around her waist (that was hidden by the jacket). She was thus transformed into a figure from mythology which

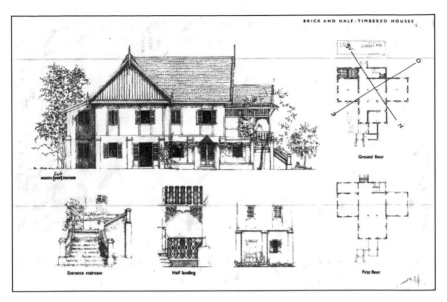

Downstream Mansion (Hong Taeuy).

stunned the bystanders. Her former suitors stood on the pavements
stupefied by this vision, as if they were contemplating an unattainable
being.

Quite different, however, was the reaction of jealous young women
of marriageable age. Far from standing watching in admiration, the
choice of Kham-Phiou as Prince Souvanna Phouma's bride, was felt as
an intolerable insult. In all innocence the young bride had let loose a
storm of hatred and jealousy, as much among her own acquaintances
as among her future in-laws.

Shortly after the departure of the procession, one of her older
female cousins, aided and abetted by a friend, pounced on the bride
to tear off her scarf:

"Take off that scarf," she said, "it does not match your outfit! Take
this one instead," holding out another.

Kham-Phiou hung on to her own scarf with all her strength crying
out, "I do not want to change!"

Bystanders, realising this was an attempt to spoil the wedding day, came to her aid and chased off the intruders, severely reprimanding them: "Why are you behaving so badly? Your jealousy is leading you to behave evilly. You are trying to cast a shadow over the marriage. Be off with you, you wicked girls!"

The procession continued on its way after this brief interruption, but it had shocked Kham-Phiou. Feeling shaken, the heavy weight of her ornaments was making the long walk to the Hong Taeuy difficult. Indeed, the route seemed unending. Sadly this was not the last of her troubles...

The Downstream Mansion was a large building standing on carved wooden piles and shaded by clumps of trees among which the elegant shapes of coconut and betel nut trees stood out.

Built to a cruciform plan, it had a pitched roof of flat, clay tiles and two outside staircases: the one at the principal gable end was built of brick and, leading directly to the reception hall, was only used on formal occasions. The other, built of wood and for everyday use, connected at the rear of the building, housing the private apartments composed of four-bedroom units, a large hall and a wide veranda, with a separate building at ground level housing the kitchen, the bathroom and toilets. This second staircase was habitually used by everyone, whether members of the princely family, visitors or domestic staff.

The usual wedding rite consisted of three parts. First the bride and groom had to take their places side by side with their respective tray of souls in front of each of them.

For the second stage, a religious representative, often a person who had spent a period as a monk[49], carried out the role of master of ceremonies (*mo phone*[50]), chanting an appeal for the return of all the souls of the bridal couple which might have wandered into other worlds and got lost, or might have succumbed to the charms of an attractive person or even been captured by evil spirits. To appease them, as well as the sweet singing of spiritual chants, they were offered all kinds of food and sweetmeats which had been placed around the base of the pyramids.

In the third stage, when all the souls were believed to have returned to their respective trays, the officiating master of ceremonies, with a gesture over the hands of the bridal couple, returned the full complement of souls to the bodies of their respective owners, then consecrated the union of the couple by tying their wrists together with a strip of cotton.

The ceremony was concluded by performing the *soma* ritual with offerings of banana-leaf cones filled with flowers and a pair of wax candles, and banana-leaf cones filled with betel-nut leaves to the elders of the family.

On this wedding day, all the doors and windows of the reception hall of the Downstream Mansion had been opened wide, giving a view over the grand staircase, the gardens and the beautiful tiered roofs of the temple of Vat That. Inside the floor was covered with mats, rugs and cushions for the event.

In the centre of the reception chamber, Souvanna Phouma dressed in a ceremonial costume of silk jacket, *sampot* and sash, sat in an armchair close to his soul elements tray, which had been prepared by the family under the attentive supervision of the lady of the house, Princess Sa-Ngiem Kham.

When Souvanna Phouma heard the singing and music announcing the approaching bridal procession, he could not restrain himself but leapt to his feet and dashed towards the grand staircase to welcome his bride. To his astonishment he found his way barred by his relatives who explained that according to tradition, his rank prohibited him from lowering his dignity in this way. Reluctantly, he returned to his armchair and awaited his bride's arrival.

Shortly afterwards, Kham-Phiou appeared, beautiful but worn down with exhaustion and distress. The elements of her own tray of souls, carried from Ban Sieng Mouane, were reassembled and placed beside that of Souvanna Phouma.

When everyone was seated in the reception hall, an unforeseen event occurred, which was deeply shocking to all those present. Instead of Souvanna Phouma being invited to take his place beside the bride, the master of ceremonies covered his tray of souls with a jacket belonging to the groom.

Such a public insult was intended to humiliate the family of Nang Kham-Phiou. Although they had been unable to prevent the marriage, Princess Sa-Ngiem Kham and her family were still hoping for more favourable circumstances and were thereby signifying that so far as they were concerned, the bride would only be a secondary wife.

Kham-Phiou, having never witnessed a similar wedding ritual felt lost, feared the worst. Souvanna Phouma, like her, understood nothing of the situation, but saw it as a tasteless masquerade. Contorted with anguish, Kham-Phiou was on the point of bursting into tears. Seeing her state, Souvanna Phouma lost his temper and stood up demanding:

"What is the meaning of this? I am the one getting married. I am sitting here!" With which he sat down in his proper place in front of his tray of souls and beside his bride.

With this total uproar broke out in the corridor behind the reception hall which led to the private apartments. Here were assembled the marriageable young cousins and nieces who had hoped to marry the prince. Their shrieks and shrill cries of pain as if they were being strangled were intermingled with odious curses as they yelled at Kham-Phiou. With a leap Souvanna Phouma reached the corridor and bluntly drove away the troublemakers.

"Who asked you to come!" he roared, "Get out, all of you!"

Faced with his fury, they fled. After calm had been restored, the ceremony was able to be celebrated according to normal rituals but given the general atmosphere of consternation it was shortened. The heart had gone out of it. The authority with which Souvanna Phouma had dealt with the situation comforted Kham-Phiou to some degree, but could not erase the memory of the miseries she had endured on what should have been the happiest day of her life,

She could not stop herself from recalling the prophecy a Siamese fortune-teller visiting Luang Prabang had made to her mother six months earlier:

"Your daughter," he had predicted, "will make a grand marriage with a prince of high birth who is himself an orphan with no mother or father. There will be a lot of hurdles to surmount but the marriage will take place. Your daughter will need to all be strong and very patient. After two or three years all will be well. The couple will be recognised and respected."

Hearing this Nang Phya Kham-Douang had laughed ironically, "I know the young eligible princes in Luang Prabang," she said, "and they all have a father and mother."

But she had forgotten Souvanna Phouma, who was indeed an orphan and had for most of his life been raised abroad.

That evening after the marriage, when the bridal couple retired to their bedroom, Souvanna Phouma did all he could to console Kham-Phiou and to make her forget the events of this dreadful day. So far as he was concerned, he was inwardly satisfied that he had achieved his aim of marrying the woman he loved. But he did genuinely regret that he had not been able to protect her, a girl of not yet seventeen who had no experience of life.

He started to tell her about many things: about France, his long journeys in mail boats from Saigon to Marseille, and the things about Laos that he had missed.

She listened attentively, interested in everything, and asking charmingly naive questions. Seeing she was now more relaxed, he ventured a compliment:

"The costume and scarf you wore for the wedding suited you so well. Were they your own choice?"

However, this unexpected reference to the ill-fated ceremony plunged Kham-Phiou into silent sadness and he could only get a simple "yes" or "no" in answer to his questions. He tried another tactic and asked her point blank:

"All those jewels you wore must have been very heavy. I was sure you were not as poor as you had implied."

Falling into the trap, Kham-Phiou's tongue was miraculously loosened.

"All those jewels do not belong to me or to my mother. For the most part they were lent for the ceremony by our aunts and cousins."

"So you have to return them?" he asked.

"Yes, tomorrow my mother will come and take them back."[51]

"Oh, then that means I have a good reason to give you some."

In fact, Kham-Phiou was able to keep a few items: a necklace, a little bracelet and everyday earrings, such items of gold jewellery as are bestowed on every child of an aristocratic family. She also kept a chain, hairpins, and flower-shaped hair ornaments, made of concentric beaten gold leaves which trembled as she moved. All these had been given to her by her aunt and adoptive mother, Nang Phya Kham-Bou, the wife of Kham-Lek Phanya Muang Kang.

Then, mentioning a future trip into the country, where he invited her to accompany him, he presented his wife with a travel toilet kit, labelled 'France'.

"Go on, open it," he told her with an amused smile.

Curious, she carefully opened it and took out in turn a deep blue glass perfume bottle labelled 'Bourjois', a powder compact, a lipstick, scented soap, a silver tumbler, toothbrushes and flannels.

Overcome with wonder at these precious novelties, Kham-Phiou played with them like a child. The atmosphere became completely relaxed and lasted till they went to bed. Souvanna Phouma felt happy.

Chapter 4

The day after the wedding

The next morning, Souvanna Phouma was determined to have it out with his elder sister regarding the appallingly vulgar behaviour of their nieces. That day the nieces, contrary to their normal habit of coming to the Downstream Mansion early in the morning to attract Souvanna Phouma's attention, did not appear. So besides the newlyweds, only the usual residents of the Mansion, Princess Sa-Ngiem Kham and her two children, the youngest of whom named Ekarath, was barely six months old and an elderly female cousin were at the meal.

Prince Souvannarath, who preferred to live with his second wife, was not present. The latter who was both half-brother and brother-in-law to Souvanna Phouma, had shown himself supportive of the marriage.

The two cooks, one belonging to the Mansion and one named Bot, whom Souvanna Phouma had recently engaged as a sort of general servant, prepared the meal.

When the food was ready, the dishes were placed on a large rattan tray and the family took their places, not in the traditional seating order (where the more important sat facing the exterior) but, at Souvanna Phouma's decree, according to French protocol. Thus his sister sat on his right and his wife on his left.

He first offered a dish to his sister and then to his wife, then served himself. After this his cousin and the older children served themselves.

Mom Kham-Phiou observed these table manners with interest and was reminded of her own parents' no less original habit. Every day two trays were prepared: one for her parents and one for the children and their nurse. This was perfectly normal. What seemed singular, even eccentric in the eyes of some, was that her parents always used their own china crockery in whatever circumstances and wherever they were, even at communal meals in temples during festivals. It was only when they were invited to the Royal Palace that they did not bring their own dishes along. The household members usually referred to the 'bowl of *nang phya*' and the 'bowl of *tiao houa*[1]' as the owners of the house were usually called by their family or neighbourhood, and a specific servant was detailed to carry the china to and from the place of the meal. No one ever understood the reason for this habit. Her father detailed a child to accompany the bearer but it was nearly always Kham-Phiou who was chosen – she was her father's favourite.

While her father was satisfied the whole week with his favourite food, the *ok lam*[2], which is a delicious combination comprising no less than a dozen kinds of vegetables, shoots and wild plants, spices and meat cooked to different degrees, Kham-Phiou for her part preferred to vary her menu with the wide choice that the typical cuisine of Luang Prabang offered. Dishes included rice vermicelli soup *(khao poun*[3]*)* in its different versions of broth, coconut milk and chili *(nam phik*[4]*)* sometimes accompanied by species of small round fungus *(hed pho*[5]*)* crunchy under the teeth, with fish sauce *(nam pa*[6]*)*, chili sauce *(nam jiaeo*[7]*)*, small egg rolls stuffed with meat and steamed *(phan khai*[8]*)*, fish mousse *(mok pa fok*[9]*)*, stuffed bamboo shoots *(oua no mai*[10]*)*, steamed vegetable shoots salad garnished with sesame seeds and ginger *(soub phak*[11]*)*, steamed young jackfruit salad *(soub mak mi*[12]*)*, eggplant melting in meat *(pon mak kheua*[13]*)*, pork rind fried with fish in brine *(khiaeo pa daek*[14]*)*, as well as all the seasonal dishes, such as the famous steamed papillotes of *dok khae*[15] flower *(mok dok khae*[16]*)*, *lin mai*[17] fruits *(mok mak lin mai*[18]*)*, or ginger buds *(mok dok khing*[19]*)*, fish eggs in brine *(som khai pa*[20]*)*, shrimps caught in Nam Nga River and smoked *(koung yang*[21]*)*, etc., all accompanied by various ginger sauces *(jiaeo khing*[22]*)*, with *mak kok*[23] fruit *(jiaeo mak kok*[24]*)*, rattan shoots *(jiaeo nyod vay*[25]*)*, chili pepper and buffalo rind *(jiaeo bong*[26]*)* that have been enjoyed for generations.

When Kham-Phiou told Souvanna Phouma of her memories, he was much amused, but also a little sad as he had never had the chance to experience close parental affection. His parents had died too early and he had also been ignored amongst the mass of brothers, sisters and half-brothers and half-sisters.

In the afternoon, Nang Phya Kham-Douang, accompanied by the *mae nom*, went to the Downstream Mansion to collect the wedding jewellery from Kham-Phiou. Princess Sa-Ngiem Kham welcomed her. She had recognised in Nang Phya Kham-Douang's strategy the mark of the proud matriarchal clan of Sieng Mouane determined not to fall under the yoke of the nobility. Had not two young women of the clan in her generation been approached in vain by the king to become his concubines?

At that time, the parents had been well aware that their daughters were not noble enough to marry a king, but were from a good enough family not to become his concubines!

The main road in Luang Prabang with Vat Mai on the left.

The princess had no reason to reproach Nang Phya Kham-Douang. On the contrary, she admired her in a certain way. For her part, Nang Phya Kham-Douang had no acrimony against the princess, whom she knew and usually met during their *phai tong* games[27] at the Royal Palace.

Like her daughter, Nang Phya Kham-Douang thought back to the words of the Siamese fortune-teller which she had imprudently mocked. In fact, she had known of the birth of Souvanna Phouma, but at a very young age he had been sent to Hanoi[28] for his primary and secondary education and then to France for his higher education. He was thus unknown in Luang Prabang. Even when his father died,[29] he did not appear. His mother had died on an unknown date. So it was quite correct that by the end of his adolescence he was an orphan.

Vat Sieng Mouane.

It was one of his elder brothers, Prince Phetsarath[30] and his wife – a rich widow – Princess Kham-Vaen, also known as 'Princess-One-Eye' because of an eye defect – who supported him financially during his graduate studies.

The second prediction of the fortune-teller was that the marriage would be full of pitfalls. This had become clear during the procession and the ceremony. It was true, Nang Phya Kham-Douang inwardly acknowledged, that she was largely responsible for trying to resist the marriage in various ways. But she had acted, she thought, for the good of her daughter, in order to spare her any later suffering.

Certainly the circumstances would have been different had she not found herself a widow so young. The status of her late husband, Tiao Phanya Luang Mun Na, allied to the Great Lineage on his mother's side, and his important functions in the French administration, would probably have counted in the matrimonial transactions and affected the attitude of the persons concerned towards her family and her daughter.

Nevertheless, if despite the obstacles and difficult ordeals, the couple had finally been able to unite, according to popular Buddhist logic, their union was the prolongation of a love lived in a former life. And if that were the case, nothing could be done about it. Souvanna Phouma seemed to love his wife sincerely and his strong personality was likely to be able to protect her in her new environment. But for how long? Under the pressure of his own family, would he not change his mind, like others had done before him?

For now, as Nang Phya Kham-Douang continued her musings, if the fortune-teller's third prediction was as accurate as the two previous ones, it was necessary for Kham-Phiou to take her courage in both hands and to arm herself with patience for two or three years, after which the couple would enjoy happiness, prosperity and celebrity.

After reminding her daughter of the politeness, deference, and helpfulness due to the inhabitants of the Mansion – the breach of which would seriously undermine her own family's reputation – Nang Phya Kham-Douang announced that she would come back every week and took leave of Princess Sa-Ngiem Kham.

Phra Bot of Vat Sieng Mouane.

She went back home by the main street, passing the majestic Vat Mai temple and the Royal Palace. Closely followed by the *mae nom* who was clasping to her breast the wedding jewellery wrapped in a canvas bag, Nang Phya Kham-Douang arrived in the Chinese Quarter (Ban Jek[31]) and took a left turn at a cross-lane which led directly to the family temple of Sieng Mouane[32], named after the melodious sound of its Great-Drum.

This building had been the object of pride and of loving care by all the family since its edification. Each generation had devoted themselves to beautifying it and a few years later, it would be her daughter, Mom Kham-Phiou, who would make the gift of the elegant wooden consoles *(khaen nang[33])* on which rest the edges of the tile roof carved by her uncle, Thid Thong-Di, and who would order a *Phra Bot[34]* in gold leaf, representing the 28 Buddhas, to decorate the wall at the back of the Great Buddha.

All these offerings were intended to acquire spiritual merits, as evidenced by the two golden stupas standing in the temple courtyard and erected by her family's ancestors.

Chapter 5

Daily life at the Downstream Mansion

Apart from the weekly visits of Nang Phya Kham-Douang, the residence regularly received visits from Princess Saeng Sourichan ('Princess Sun-and-Moon- Rays'). Born in 1889 to Viceroy Bounkhong and his second wife, Princess Kham-Vaen, she was the half-sister of Souvanna Phouma and his elder by twelve years. She had an unusual destiny for a woman of her time.

At the age of two, she was taken to Bangkok during the reign of King Chulalongkorn together with a small group of noble children of the Front Lineage, accompanied by their nurses.

At the age of six, she entered the Siamese Palace School to undertake primary schooling. Three years later, in 1898, Prince Bounkhong, wishing to repatriate her to Luang Prabang, thanks to the support of Auguste Pavie[1] obtained permission to remove her from the Royal Palace and placed her at the Catholic Assumption School for a year. Then she was taken to Vietnam and entrusted to the École de la Sainte Enfance, in Saigon, where her father, on an official visit, met her again. By the time of her return to Luang Prabang in 1900, she had acquired a wide knowledge of the outside world, spoke French and Siamese and could speak English and Vietnamese reasonably well.

Just as her childhood was eventful, her private life as an adult was no less so. She had three husbands; the first, whom she married in her seventeenth year, in 1906, died five years later; the second in 1914 bored her to such an extent that in 1917 she took leave of the school where she had taught for two years to undertake training as a teacher at the French École Primaire Supérieure de Jeunes Filles in Saigon.

In 1920, the year of her father's death, she returned to Luang Prabang with her first-class teachers diploma and set up a girls' school[2]. It was at this establishment that Kham-Phiou learned to read.

The following year, after divorcing her second husband, she remarried for the third time with Prince Chittarath, a teacher like her, who was her own half-brother and the eldest of Souvanna Phouma's siblings. Because of Saeng Sourichan's reputation as a 'modern woman', Princess Thong-Sy, Chittarath's mother, was not in favour of their union, but the couple ignored her advice. This last marriage was for Saeng Sourichan the love of her life. Alas, in 1928, Chittarath died without giving her a child.

The princess had not forgotten Kham-Phiou, the youngest student at the opening of her school. Entered at the age of six, she learned in two years to read and write Lao fluently and retained a considerable number of French terms. The decision of Nang Phya Kham-Douang to remove her daughter from school and to pay for private lessons at home on the grounds that she would become too intelligent and independent, saddened the teacher who believed in her pupil's potential.

Now she joyfully met her again in her own family, united to Souvanna Phouma in a deep and sincere love like the one she herself had experienced during her late husband's lifetime. Already half-sister of Souvanna Phouma by birth, she became sister-in-law to Mom Kham-Phiou by marriage.

Notwithstanding the great affection she felt for Mom Kham-Phiou, the real object of Princess Saeng Sourichan's visits to the Mansion was surprisingly the youngest of Princess Sa-Ngiem Kham's children.

It is said that on the day of Prince Chittarath's funeral, before closing the coffin, Princess Saeng Sourichan had marked her husband's abdomen with the reddish juice of a betel chew in order to recognise him in his next life. It just so happened that on the day of his birth, the lastborn of Princess Sa-Ngiem Kham had a mark in exactly the same place. Certain that she had found her late husband, on each visit, she felt consolation and happiness from looking at and playing with the young boy.

Later, when the child began to speak, she told him: "You were Chittarath in your previous existence, so you are still Chittarath in this current life." To her astonishment the child answered back: "Not Chittarath, Ekarath!"

Ekarath means 'independent'. When he grew up, the child wanted to become a soldier and he later achieved this by undertaking brilliant studies at Saint-Cyr Military School in France.

According to tradition, once married a girl must remove her anklets. But Souvanna Phouma, despite frequent reminders from Princess Sa-Ngiem Kham, was unwilling for them to be removed and continually delayed. He was sentimentally attached to his first memories of Kham-Phiou and in particular to the chink made by the heavy, crescent-shaped, chased solid silver anklets as she walked.

After a few weeks, however, in response to a last injunction from his elder sister, he gave way. The operation, consisting of pulling apart the ends of the jewel anklets so as to free the ankle, took place on the main veranda. The method, although unexpected, was very simple. One of the ends was tied to a pillar by a cord while the other cord was pulled by Bot, the cook. Souvanna Phouma was following the work with obvious nostalgia. When the first anklet was freed by Bot's efforts, it left a mark.

'Look,' cried one observer, 'a mark!'

This remark immediately brought Souvanna Phouma back to the present and he commented that these anklets were designed to stop girls chasing boys, a joke that caused a general laugh.

At that time, Lao society was governed by a strict code of etiquette laying down rules for the appropriate behaviour between different ranks and ages. Respect due to a person of a higher rank, or senior in age, social class or office translated into appropriate bodily stances: whether bowing, bending or kneeling according to the person's respective status and circumstances. The most important rule was never to be higher than the head of a superior.

Kham-Phiou had been trained in this code by her mother since her childhood and as the eldest sister had herself benefitted from it.

By contrast in the mansion her age and non-noble social background meant that she was in the lowest position of all. In this new environment she was obliged to always watch her every movement to ensure she did not infringe this code. Souvanna Phouma found this traditional social etiquette obsolete and inappropriate for his wife. It was particularly difficult to observe this rule if a superior was seated, as was usual on the floor and one had to pass him or her. It meant crawling past on hands and knees.

One day when Kham-Phiou was crawling past Princess Sa-Ngiem Kham who was seated on a mat, surrounded by nieces and cousins, he went to lift her up declaring in exasperation: "There is no need to crawl, it damages one's knees, bowing is quite sufficient."

Taken aback by his spontaneous outburst, the princess remained silent. Seeing their aunt's silence, the nieces also held their tongues but their fury at seeing Kham-Phiou benefit from another example of Souvanna Phouma's assertion of his wife's standing and his consideration for her certainly did not abate. Kham-Phiou was apprehensive of such moments, realising that every time her husband leapt to her defence, she paid a heavy price the moment he was absent.

The following day towards the end of the afternoon when people took their daily bath, Souvanna Phouma was chatting peacefully with his family on the veranda while awaiting his turn. As Kham-Phiou came back from the bathing area, her towel over her shoulders, as a joke he grabbed it as she passed. Taken by surprise, Kham-Phiou could not catch it back.

"Lend me your towel," he called to her, "I too am going to take a shower."

However, according to Lao custom, a man may not use a woman's linen nor may she use a man's. Souvanna Phouma was showing his affection for Kham-Phiou in defying this convention.

As he spoke one of his nieces had a fit of hysterics, screaming insults at Kham-Phiou, and calling down curses on her as she had done at the marriage ceremony. She addressed her using vulgar and condescending speech to signify that Kham-Phiou did not deserve all these attentions.

This time Souvanna Phouma looked at his niece calmly and said coldly:

"It is you who are not worthy of it!"

Suddenly aware of the enormity of her conduct, the young woman fled the scene and did not show her face at the Mansion for several weeks.

A few days later, the momentary absence of Souvanna Phouma gave an opportunity for Kham-Phiou's detractors to take revenge for the collective humiliation they had suffered with their aunt.

They subjected her to a storm of mockery, spitefulness and insane criticism which only ended with Souvanna Phouma's unexpected appearance.

"Come Kham-Phiou," he said in a voice loud enough to carry clearly to the family gathering, "don't remain here to listen to their nasty and vulgar words."

This episode had not only hurt Kham-Phiou very deeply but also humiliated and disgusted her. So much united vulgarity and spitefulness was unbearable to her and led to the couple's first argument. She accused Souvanna Phouma of having only married her in order to subject her to this intolerable situation.

Souvanna Phouma reiterated his love and affection and advised her to pay no attention to their remarks. However, while he was able to react with scorn and to counter their behaviour Kham-Phiou, only sixteen, was a stranger in the family, and brought up in an atmosphere of courtesy and good manners, felt helpless. Trying to give her courage, Souvanna Phouma emphasised the scorn which his relatives' behaviour inspired in him by using a current crude expression: "Receive their remarks with your backside, don't pay attention to them!"[3]

"You know," he continued, "they always hoped to marry me so now they are doing everything possible to upset you and to divide us by making you quarrel with me."

He also exhorted his wife to respond to them in kind, with equal insolence but Kham-Phiou's upbringing made this impossible. It was not in her nature.

As we shall learn, the daily presence of the nieces in the Downstream

Mansion as well as their freedom of behaviour and language in expressing their profound frustration and their fierce opposition to Kham-Phiou, was due to an arrangement concluded long ago between their parents and Princess Sa-Ngiem Kham to marry them to Souvanna Phouma. There were few eligible men of adequate status for the three nieces and they had remained unmarried, awaiting Souvanna Phouma's return.

This arrangement, however, which had been concluded without informing Souvanna Phouma had not taken into consideration his independence of character nor the influence on him of western ideas. Quite apart from the fact that he had fallen in love with Kham-Phiou, he had no intention of being married to any of the nieces. Nevertheless, despite apparently thwarting his elder sister's plans by marrying a girl of his own choice, as in Lao society a noble could marry more than one wife, this first marriage did not settle the matter so far as his sister was concerned.

One afternoon, one of Souvanna Phouma's nieces asked Kham-Phiou to help her finish a wedding dress. Kham-Phiou helped her unquestioningly despite feeling some apprehension.

"This is my wedding dress," said the niece. "We shall be living together."

On hearing such words, Kham-Phiou's heart began to beat wildly.

"Of course," continued the niece with relentless brutality, "although you married the prince before me, as a noble woman, I shall of course take precedence as his principal wife."

Kham-Phiou felt the ground giving way beneath her, but, summoning all her strength, said nothing and continued to sew as if nothing was wrong, holding back the tears that were threatening to fall. Meanwhile, she thought to herself: "Should that day ever come, I shall simply leave here without any argument or explanation."

That evening she remained in her room, refusing to attend dinner. To her husband she seemed to be in another world. Despite questioning her repeatedly, she made no response. Souvanna Phouma appreciated that the situation was very serious and realised that she must have yet again been the victim of abuse from his nieces. But in what way?

Pressed to answer and explain, Kham-Phiou finally wept scalding tears and described what had happened.

Souvanna Phouma was distressed to see her in this state and furious beyond measure at the cruel, and dishonest behaviour of his niece. She had gone too far, and he promised himself he would deal with the situation once and for all.

He also reassured Kham-Phiou that he would never marry any of his nieces because of consanguinity and the risk of giving birth to physically or mentally handicapped children as had happened in some families. Because of his education in France, he was aware of the problem and disapproved of this kind of alliance within his own family. Even more specifically he reiterated that he did not like any of them.

"I knew them before I met you and on the day of my arrival in Luang Prabang, they were already strutting before me. If any of them had attracted me, I would have married them then, especially since their parents did not even require a dowry," he added convincingly.

His reassuring words were like balm to Kham-Phiou's sore heart. She believed in his sincerity but she still doubted his ability to deal with the problem. The wickedness and perversity of the nieces was such that she could not imagine a happy outcome.

As the couple discussed the situation in their room, the nieces, exalted by the new situation created at the expense of Kham-Phiou, began to dream of their future, spending hours imagining the most incredible scenarios of marriage with Souvanna Phouma. When they had finished, feeling sleepy, they decided, as was their habit when the night was late, to sleep in the private hall.

The next day Souvanna Phouma rose early and with a stern face. The sight of his nieces sleeping on mattresses sprawled in front of his bedroom, a situation he had hitherto tolerated, was now unacceptable to him. He roared out, "What are so many people doing in this house? It is impossible to live here."

The effect was immediate. Woken suddenly from sleep, his nieces took off, crouching down with heads bowed, leaving their bedding behind.

Souvanna Phouma, as a prospecting officer on behalf of the Société d'Études et d'Exploitations Minières de l'Indochine (SEEMI[4]), regularly visited places in the vicinity of Luang Prabang. In order to shield his wife from his family's intolerable harassment, he decided to take her with him on his long trips away.

For the first time in her life, Kham-Phiou discovered the countryside. Until then she had known only Luang Prabang and Vientiane, where she had spent much of her childhood until the death of her father. This discovery proved to be a real delight for her. Everything seemed beautiful and peaceful and she was able to regain her childlike carefreeness and joy of living.

However, if it was only a short trip Souvanna Phouma left her behind at the Mansion in the hope that she would be forced to defend herself. Sadly, Kham-Phiou made no progress in this field. As soon as the prince had left, her torturers again began their malicious harassment, more cautiously it is true, but now knowing how best to hurt her, they managed to make her suffer unbearably. The result was that when Souvanna Phouma came back he had to use all his inventive powers to distract his wife, to turn her thoughts away from her miseries and to reconcile her to the absence which had led to it.

One day, having run out of arguments, he had the idea of playing a practical joke on her.

"Come and see," he said, showing, her an oil lamp which lit the room. "There is a scarab which lights fires."[5]

This old chestnut was applied, no one can say why, to people who sulk. Not knowing this joke, Kham-Phiou looked closely at the lamp and its surroundings. Seeing nothing she looked at her husband questioningly. Pleased with his trick, Souvanna Phouma pointed his index finger at Kham-Phiou's forehead, saying, "the scarab is here" and bursting out laughing. Caught out and ashamed, Kham-Phiou blushed, while secretly admiring her husband for his knowledge of their traditional culture.

A few days later Souvanna Phouma was summoned by his elder sister to a private meeting. Kham-Phiou who had now become watchful, observed them from her room and when Princess Sa-Ngiem Kham began to speak, she put her ear to a crack so as to overhear every word.

The princess began: "I have summoned you to discuss an important subject. Now you have married and fulfilled the promise you made, you must think about your nieces. You can choose one or all three of them." Flabbergasted by such a proposal, Souvanna Phouma made a categorical refusal.

"No, I do not wish to marry anyone else: I am already married."

"But do you realise their family has huge lands so that their inheritance will be substantial?" pointed out the princess.

"No, I am not willing to marry another wife," interrupted Souvanna Phouma. Then, ostentatiously rubbing his hands together in front of his sister, he added: "My fortune lies in the hollow of these hands." By that he meant that he would earn his own living, independent of any inheritance. And that was the end of the interview.

From this time on, Princesse Sa-Ngiem Kham seemed to accept that Souvanna Phouma would never marry any of the nieces. Never having anticipated that her younger brother would not, as was customary, accept her settling his marriage, she had agreed one in his absence and was now in a difficult position with regard to her nieces and their family with whom she had concluded the understanding. The nieces, who had been willing to wait to marry Souvanna Phouma while he completed his studies, were now in their twenties and unlikely to find other husbands even though it was clear that it would be impossible for her to honour her agreement.

Souvanna Phouma's words fully corroborated his declarations to Kham-Phiou some days earlier. As well as giving emotional and genetic reasons for not wishing to marry his nieces, on this occasion he declared his scorn for their fortune and confirmed his absolute decision not to marry further. His firm stance and reiterated position swept away Kham-Phiou's doubts. Now convinced of the total sincerity of his feelings towards her, she felt immensely grateful to him and loved him all the more. She also now understood that, unbeknownst to Souvanna Phouma, there had been a longstanding tacit agreement between the families concerned to marry the nieces to him.

Chapter 6

Stories of Gold

The new situation of trust had created an excellent understanding between the young couple and they enjoyed telling each other about their respective family histories. Souvanna Phouma began with an account of the life of his grandfather, Prince Souvanna Phomma, whose mother named Khao was a commoner. Because of her kindness and to show his gratitude and affection for her, when he became Viceroy in 1878, he elevated her to the rank of 'Sathou Nying Khao' (Princess Khao). As he recounted this procedure which was common in at the Court of Siam, but unique in the history of the royal lineages of Luang Prabang, was Souvanna Phouma cherishing the hope of ennobling his own wife, to give her a title which would put her beyond the reach of her torturers? Kham-Phiou dared not dream of this.

By way of response she recounted a story dating back three generations:

"One day my great-grandfather Kham-Ouane had gone fishing in the Mekong, downstream of Luang Prabang.

"He had not noticed the current had swept away his pirogue out. He could only reach the banks by rowing then pulling the boat upstream to its original position. On the way the metal tip of his pole caught in the bank causing a slight ringing. Surprised, he examined the tip and found a tiny golden speck. He went nearer to see what it was and was astounded to discover a gold nugget below the water. It was as big as a coconut! He took care to mark the exact spot and went home to tell his wife of his incredible find. Next day, equipped with fishing rods to avoid arousing the suspicions of the neighbourhood, but also carrying a pickaxe and a strong jute sack, they both went to collect the treasure and brought it back discreetly."

"It's interesting," said Souvanna Phouma, "that reminds of the legend of Chanthaphanit. He also found gold at the end of his pole while sailing upstream the Mekong, and it's in the same place!"

"Yes," replied Kham-Phiou, "I also thought of that!"

According to legend, Chanthaphanit was a modest but very pious betel merchant from the Vientiane region. After a dream, interpreted by a former monk, Maha Thaen, as being highly auspicious, he went to Luang Prabang on a pirogue with a group of relatives and friends. On reaching the Tad Kae cliff[1], downstream of the city, their poles got caught on gold rocks.

But in accordance with Maha Thaen's recommendations, they threw the gold back into the water. When they reached the upper end of the large sandbank facing the mouth of the Nam Khan River, the rocks turned into gold. Nevertheless, they were only allowed to take the gold after a period of eight days. Seeing such a miracle, and convinced of they were dealing with a person of great merit, the population built a palace at the confluence of the Mekong and its tributary, the Nam Khan. While clearing the ground for this, a large quantity of gold was also found. Chanthaphanit used it during his long reign to make the people very prosperous.

Another version of the origin of the family wealth, known as 'The Story of the Jar of Silver and, the Jar of Gold', told by Nang Sao, a first cousin of Mom Kham-Phiou, recounted that: "One day, our great-grandfather, Kham-Ouane, was coming back from Vientiane on his boat, laden with the sacks of salt which he traded, when feeling tired during the afternoon, he moored on the bank of Mekong to take a rest. He had the following dream: an old man, dressed in white – probably a hermit or a *thevada*[2] (deity) – came down from the mountain asking him, 'Who are you and where do you come from?' Our great-grandfather replied: 'I come from the town of the Lords [Luang Prabang]. The old man persisted: 'Where is the city of the Lords?' Our great-grandfather said, 'The city of the Lords is to the north'.

"Then the old man exclaimed, 'Oh, I am already old, and I have something for you, take it with you to gain merit for me!' Great-grandfather Kham-Ouane asked, 'Where is it?'. The old man said, 'It is where you dug in your pole.'

"When he woke up, great-grandfather Kham-Ouane went to the indicated place and rummaged in the sand with the tip of his pole. He then discovered a large stone resting on a jar filled with silver and on another filled with gold. Silver and gold were in the form of plates stacked one on top of the other. He told his travelling companions – each one had his own boat – that he was still tired and would not leave yet. He waited for twilight to tip the salt into the water and to fill the empty sacks with the silver and gold. He left only two sacks of salt, one at each end of the boat and placed the other seven sacks filled with gold and silver in the middle. At nightfall, he slowly ascended the Mekong to the pier of Ban Sieng Mouane.

"In accordance with his dream, from that day on great-grandfather Kham-Ouane made religious offerings and acquired merit according to *hid 12 khong 14*[3] *('the 12 uses and 14 customs')*."

The two golden stupas in Vat Sieng Mouane.

This version differed somewhat from hers, but whatever it may be, continued Kham-Phiou, "From then on our family enjoyed great prosperity. My great-grandparents, considering the discovery as a gift from heaven, lived a modest life but made sumptuous gifts to their family temples of Vat Pa Phai[4] and Vat Sieng Mouane with the two golden stupas as well as the great stupa above the sacred hill of Phousi in the centre of Luang Prabang, and the Mak Mo (Water Melon) stupa of Vat Vixun[5].

"These gifts were offered on the occasion of the annual festivals of the Buddhist calendar, such as *boun phra vet*[6] on the first month of the lunar calendar, the Vessantara festival to celebrate the last life of Prince Vessantara before his enlightenment as a Buddha; or *boun kanthin*[7] in the eleventh month of the lunar calendar, consisting of donations of new robes for the monks after the rainy season. These offerings could also take place on personal occasions such as celebrating one's birthday, or prolonging one's own life *(bouad phra khou anyou*[8]*)* by sponsoring a number of individuals, equal in number to one's age plus one, to undertake a period as monks on the eighth month of the lunar calendar before the monsoon or on the consecration of a meritorious monk *(bouad kong hod*[9]*)*.

"Each day at sunrise after the monk's collection of food offerings along the roads, our family provided food for the two daily meals at the temple prescribed by the monastic rule; the first at 7 am and the second at 11 am. As Vat Sieng Mouane was close by, this was simple via direct access from the family's house, but Vat Pa Phai was some way away by a roundabout route. Our ancestor therefore created a path through his orchard. This lane through coconut trees, areca trees, and all kinds of fruit trees, was said to be very agreeable and had the extra advantage of a small bamboo bridge with a view over the Khi Mot stream[10].

"At each traditional New Year celebration they slipped into each monk's daily begging bowl a fragment of gold in addition to the rice, 2 *salung*[11] to each monk and 1 *salung*[12] to each novice. Nor did they forget the poor, donating rice at times of famine and covers in cold winters or years of food shortage. In addition, their house remained open to all passers-by. They could always find food cooked at home, a practice called 'tray of food served in the middle of the home'[13], as well as clothes for both women and men. Common prisoners could also benefit from these donations.

"Upon the death of his wife, my great-grandfather invited all the monks of the city to her funeral, and offered each of them a gold plate worth 1 baht[14] (15 g). It was also an opportunity for him to cancel the debt of all their debtors.

"The generosity of my great-grandparents extended beyond the family: many families who entered as slaves in the household were subsequently freed. They were treated gently and with much affection as the Lao custom required and their daughters were richly endowed and made good marriages with young officials.

"At the same time my great-grandparents increased their financial means by sending out agents to buy goods from neighbouring areas – earthenware and lacquered boxes from Burma, monk's robes and kitchen items from Siam to which at the end of the rainy season they added silks, furs, felt carpets and fine china brought by the Chinese caravans from Sichuan and Yunnan Provinces. All of these goods were divided into lots and sold from home by my great-grandmother. In addition, the household kept a set of blue-and-white porcelain and copper items reserved for religious ceremonies, which the neighbourhood could also borrow.

"The merits of my great-grandfather were recognised by the Royal Palace and he was rewarded with the honorific title of Tiao Phanya Sisonsay, commonly known as Tiao Phanya Setthi Sieng Mouane ('Lord-Millionaire-of-Sieng Mouane') and my great-grandmother, whose name was Chan Nya, became Nang Phya Chan Nya. They built the family temple of Vat Sieng Mouane[15].

"I told you that my great-grand parents lived modest lives. That is true. But I must tell you that my great-grandmother had an amusing passion, namely for silk skirts and scarves. Each time she went out she put on new ones while taking great care not to spoil them. On her

Vat Pa Phai.

return home, in accordance with the practices of the time, she exposed the reverse side to the sun before storing them, carefully folded, in a rattan trunk. On her death, her daughters inherited an impressive number of skirts and scarves, each more lovely than the last, their colours still as fresh as new."

Souvanna Phouma seemed very interested in Kham-Phiou's tale. He also felt she possessed a real gift as a narrator or story teller.

"Where do you get this gift from?" he asked her.

"I love our traditional tales, those found in mulberry leaf manuscripts and written in *tham*[16] scripture, called *nang su phouk*[17], especially 'Kalaket'[18], 'Souvat'[19], 'In Nao'[20], 'Phouthasen'[21] and others. I listened to all of them avidly when a child, and later I was asked to read them on the eve of religious or private festivals."

Souvanna Phouma was familiar with these classics full of different episodes, romances and spiritual reflections and he too appreciated them. His curiosity however fixed on a particular point.

"Athough men generally learn to read and write during their time in the temple, today most women still remain illiterate. When and how did you come to learn?"

"It was at the wish of my father. At the age of six I was accepted by the School for Girls, which your half-sister, Princess Saeng Sourichan opened in 1920. Two years later when I had learned to read and write Lao correctly, and could stammer some French, my mother withdrew me from the school on the grounds that if I continued my head would be likely to burst! From then on, I had a private tutor at home.

"In fact, as one of my aunts told me later, my mother was afraid that if I went on with my schooling, I would have risked, as frequently Lao women did when they returned from studying abroad, losing our values and tradition."

Souvanna Phouma shook his head without making any comment and asked his wife to continue the account of her family history. She went on:

"After the good fortune of my great- grandparents, my grandparents, Phanya Kham-Di, who was given the title of Tiao Phanya Setthi

Sieng Mouane after his father-in-law, and Nang Phya Thong-Sy, experienced great misfortune when a severe fire ravaged all the upstream area of Luang Prabang. All the beautiful timber houses were burned, including their nine-room dwelling, which extended from Ban Pak Houay to the limit of Sieng Mouane temple, including Ban Pa Phai and the coconut plantation, and the small bamboo bridge crossing Houay Khi Mot stream.

A substantial part of their treasure (gold jewellery, silver bars and coins) stored underneath in the basement almost melted into the ground as a result of the intense heat.

Everything had to be rebuilt on a smaller scale. At that time, the land had already been shared out among all the children, and my grandmother Thong-Sy, probably being an elder daughter, and her husband grandfather, Kham-Di, received the part adjoining the temple of Sieng Mouane. Grandfather Kham-Di therefore ordered the construction of a rather large wooden house, although obviously more modest than that of his parents-in-law. A specific requirement was to excavated the ground so that the roof of his house was not higher than that of the temple, and also because he was afraid of storms, sometime violent in Luang Prabang.

During the period of the Siamese protectorate over Luang Prabang[22], the Siamese administration borrowed money from Grandfather Kham-Di to pay its local officials. It was his son-in-law Thid Kham-Oun, the husband of his eldest daughter, Nang Kham-Boua, and the latter's younger brother, Thid Thong-Di, who were in charge of going to Siam to be reimbursed for the sum loaned in the form of gold. Two months were necessary to complete this journey.

Grandfather Kham-Di also constructed a building on one of his plots of lands on a slope of the Phousi, which is now the police station, opposite the evening market. He made it into a small 'family casino', with each of the children and grandchildren receiving 150 *man*[23] of silver to play and learn financial management. Those who lost had to return the money to him. The most common games were *pou-pa*[24] ('crab-fish'), and *tham thoua*[25] ('do the beans'). The tokens were cowries worth

1 cent. Later grandfather donated this building and the land to the city.

"Then a second misfortune struck our family. Continuing the tradition of their parents, at the beginning of the cold season of 1898, they prepared the great festival of Phra Vet at Sieng Mouane temple. As was the case every year, young girls from our family and close families in the quarter, dressed in ceremonial attire and adorned with sumptuous jewels by my grandmother, were charged to go and announce the event to the personalities of the city. At the end of the day, one of them, named Kham-Sao[26], was lured by a relative into her house and killed in order to steal her jewellery. She was only sixteen. His Majesty Sakarin[27] enforced the punishment prescribed by the customary law to the murderer – she was put into a jute sack, weighed down with large stones, and drowned in the current of the Mekong. The memory of this sad story has survived to this day in our family.

"At the beginning of 1900, after the death of our grandmother, our grandfather wished to remarry a young woman from the Xieng Thong Quarter. Fearing that the family fortunes, already reduced by the fire, would fall into the hands of the future wife, my mother's elder sister, Aunt Kham-Boua with the help of her husband and servants, loaded what she estimated to be her fair share of the gold, silver and china onto the backs of four elephants. Armed only with a sabre to protect her treasure, she left and went to settle in the region of Chiang Mai in the north of Siam, where her parents owned teak forests. She was never to return to Luang Prabang. Like her ancestors, she was also famed for her habit of using only her own china, whether at home or outside, carried by a servant.

"However, in the early 1920s the family was still wealthy enough to be able to organise a grand marriage that stood out in Luang Prabang between Nang Kham-La, the youngest of the family and Kham-Pheng, an aristocrat from Ban Xieng Thong. The bride was then 18 years old and her future husband being some ten years older was, at that time, considered to be very old for marriage.

"The family of the bride had nevertheless accepted the marriage

Kham-Pheng, Tiao Phanya Na Neua with his wife Tiao Kham-Phiou
(sister of Queen Kham-Phoui's grandmother) and children; on his left, Kham-Phoui,
later Tiao Phanya Luang Mun Na, father of Mom Kham-Phiou

as Nang Kham-La was motherless, and moreover, although his prefix
'*kham*' was only recent[28], her future husband already held the title of
Phya Kom Phon and practiced as a judge in the provinces. In such
circumstances, the 'procession on both sides' took place.

On the morning of the ceremony, the bridegroom went to Ban
Sieng Mouane, then in the afternoon the bride went in procession to
her husband's house. Being the youngest of the family, she was both
spoilt and pampered as well as ravishingly beautiful. She was so loaded
with ornaments and jewellery, including the heavy gold bracelets *pok
khaen si mak louk*[29] and *pok khaen saek kiaeng saek koud*[30], that she
required a person on either side to support her during the procession.
The couple stayed in the house of the bride's parents in Ban Xieng
Thong for three days, after which they returned to the bride's home
in Ban Sieng Mouane. The couple slept in separate rooms. One night,
when her husband wanted to visit her, he found himself literally
kicked out of her room by Nang Phya Kham-La. The latter clearly had
no inclination for her 'old' husband!"

The behaviour of Aunt Kham-Boua and Aunt Kham-La made Souvanna Phouma immediately think of their sister, Nang Phya Kham-Douang, who had become his mother-in-law, but he made no mention of this to Kham-Phiou. Had he done so she would have immediately revealed to him her mother's love of music. Given that it was socially impossible for her to play an instrument or perform, Nang Phya Kham-Douang circumvented the prohibition by sponsoring a small traditional Lao orchestra available at any moment for her sole pleasure. This helped to enhance the reputation for eccentricity enjoyed by the women of the Sieng Mouane Quarter that was already widespread among the good society of Luang Prabang. This was, however, the least of her worries.

Souvanna Phouma now had confirmation of the reputation enjoyed by the women of the Sieng Mouane Quarter, of possessing both pride and strength. They were ready to spurn the wishes of the king to take their daughters as concubines, while many other families dreamed of such a chance. Furthermore, the history of Kham-Phiou's family convinced Souvanna Phouma that despite the drastic reduction in their fortune, the inheritors of Kham-Phiou's grandparents were still comfortably off. It was obvious to him that the difficulties his mother-in-law had raised, in particular the enormous bride price and pension which she had demanded, were in fact simply measures to discourage him. But, he thought, smiling to himself, she had not been able to achieve her goal.

Chapter 7

Mining prospecting in Muang Khay district

The district of Muang Khay is located 15 km south of Luang Prabang, on the bank of the Mekong River.

The journey in a pirogue took a half day rowing downstream and one day being towed upstream. Apart from Souvanna Phouma and Kham-Phiou, the expedition included the indispensable Bot, the cook and two oarsmen. They lodged in the house of the headman of Muang Khay district. He was the fortunate owner of the best and largest house on stilts in the village, characterised by two parallel roofs covered with flat clay tiles. This kind of traditional house is called a 'double house' *(heuan khou[1])*.

The day before their arrival, the headman had informed the spirit of the house of their visit, making offerings of candles, flowers and incense sticks. These offerings were for the spirit of the ancestor who had had the house built. The ceremony not only permitted the guests to stay in the house but ensured protection for them as well as their hosts.

Two new mattresses and pillows stuffed with kapok were laid in the large reception room for the couple. According to custom, the two mattresses were laid alongside each other but apart to conform to the tradition that husband and wife should not share the same mattress in another person's house.

Before leaving for the journey Souvanna Phouma had taught his wife how to prepare their luggage, in particular bringing the bedding that their hosts would not supply: pillowcases, sheets and mosquito nets. The cotton quilts which were the pride of the village of Muang Khay and its neighbouring villages would be purchased on the spot.

At daybreak, Souvanna Phouma accompanied by Bot and porters, began his prospecting on a perimeter from Muang Khay (via Ban Ou and Ban Paksy) to the district of Muang Met, inland. Kham-Phiou also rose early to steam the sticky rice, soaked in water over night, destined for the monks' morning alms round. Every three days she used concentrated starch in the remaining water to make a traditional shampoo. After an application of about ten minutes, she rinsed her superb hair in cold water and then applied, as a conditioner, a heady decoction of fresh kaffir lime.

Appropriate days for hair washing were the first, third, sixth, eleventh and thirteenth days of the waxing and waning moon, unless they fell on a Thursday. The best days were the third and sixth days, provided they corresponded to a Tuesday or a Friday. The same auspicious days were applicable for cutting nails, unless they fell on a Wednesday. When Souvanna Phouma, who was always interested but sceptical, saw his wife busy in her preparations, he would ask mockingly, 'So, it's a good day?'

During the day, Kham-Phiou divided her time between listening to the village women talking about their daily life, and answering their questions in return, accompanying them to the temple and buying handmade goods from them - tobacco to make cigarettes for her husband, traditional cotton skirts, and items of bamboo or rattan such as boxes for sticky rice or baskets. Following Souvanna Phouma's advice, she took care to make purchases from different people so as to make everyone content.

This was a wonderful period for Kham-Phiou. The gentle, shaded atmosphere of the village with its soft breezes, positioned between the forest and river echoed the harmony which Kham-Phiou now felt with the women of the village. On one side was her beauty, bearing and natural grace, on the other their admiration mixed with pride in sharing moments of exceptional intimacy.

Kham-Phiou bought supplies from the village: meat, fish and

vegetables as available which Bot then cooked on his return. Because of the strict taboo on killing animals on the eighth and fifteenth days of the waxing and waning moon, there was no meat or fish on sale on the following days.

Bot dealt with this by disappearing, gun in hand, into the forest and soon reappearing with a partridge, pheasant or wild hen. An excellent cook, he succeeded in preparing two or three dishes from one bird. Kham-Phiou truly admired his culinary gifts. Although she did not supervise the preparation of the meals, she nevertheless made sure that once the table was cleared, the cutlery used to cook or to eat did not remain soaking in the pots or the bowls, because according to popular belief, this could lead to poverty for the whole family. In the same way it was forbidden to wash the dishes at nightfall so as not to make a noise which would disturb spirits.

As was customary throughout the country, at the end of the afternoon the entire population went down to the riverside to bathe, the men upstream and the women downstream according to custom. This was also a chance to relax, to enjoy oneself and collect water for household needs. The women wore bathing skirts which are longer than the normal skirts so as to cover their bodies from breast to calf.

After his long and tiring journeys prospecting, Souvanna Phouma appreciated these moments of relaxation when he rejoined his wife. Kham-Phiou enjoyed her favourite game, known to all young Lao girls as *ti mak poum phong loy nam*[2], which consisted of forming an airpocket inside the bathing skirt by throwing water at it and thus forming a sort of billowing lifebelt enabling them to float or drift along with the water flow.

From his place among the men, Souvanna Phouma watched with a feeling of tenderness as his wife frolicked in the river. Seeing her so happy, he let her prolong her bathing. But one day when she had stayed bathing even later than usual, he decide to use a ruse to get her out and called out: "Quick, come out, there is a *ngeuak*[3] behind you!"

A *ngeuak* is a serpent-like water spirit who eats men and is a lover of pretty women, whom he drags down to his palace under the water to make them his wives. According to common belief, merely saying its name near water can make it appear.

Terrified, Kham-Phiou hastened out of the water but when her husband's burst out laughing, she realised he was teasing her to get her out of the water and her fear turned to vexation. To placate her he tried to convince her that the *ngeuak* was only a legendary creature with no actual existence. Although she didn't believe him, in future Kham-Phiou took care not to spend too long in the river.

Chapter 8

Return to Luang Prabang

On their departure from Muang Khay, despite the protestations of the village headman, Souvanna Phouma was scrupulous in paying for the headman's hospitality and the cost of the mattresses.

The return journey required two pirogues, one for the travellers and their goods and presents, the other for pebbles collected during his prospecting. After a long journey being towed upstream, the flotilla reached its destination.

Their stay in Muang Khay had allowed Souvanna Phouma to reflect more on the fraught relationship between his wife and his nieces, and he reached the conclusion that the best solution would be to promote good relations between them. So, changing his strategy, he had asked Kham-Phiou to choose presents for the women of the Downstream Mansion.

Princess Sa-Ngiem Kham was presented with a pretty container for sticky rice which pleased her, but the three nieces sneered at the sight of the cotton skirts chosen for them, as cotton in their eyes was an inferior material. Their ill-bred reaction did not affect Kham-Phiou, who was so full of anticipation at seeing her mother again. She left without delay for her mother's neighbourhood, carrying seasonal fruits, and small presents.

In the general atmosphere of welcome and rejoicing, she enthusiastically described in detail the journey by pirogues, daily life in the village, the beauty of the scenery and kindness of the villagers. She was so happy among her circle of relatives and friends that she forgot the time and did not return to the mansion in time for dinner.

When she only returned at dusk Souvanna Phouma was openly annoyed:

"Why have you been away so long?" he demanded in an angry voice, adding "Do you still need to suck at your mother's breast?"

The next day, everyday life resumed at the Mansion but something had changed, the atmosphere was more relaxed – was it a belated reaction to yesterday's presents or was it more probably the result of another initiative from Souvanna Phouma?

In fact, as a result of overnight reflection, he had asked his nieces, under threat of his displeasure, to introduce Kham-Phiou to the game of *phai tong* and had distributed money to each player.

Unlike her mother who had become devoted to the game after the death of her husband, Kham-Phiou only discovered it for the first time at Hong Taeuy. Her initiation began that afternoon with the identification of the cards, the way to hold them in her hand, followed by beginning to learn the game and its rules. Despite lapses of memory, awkwardness and mistakes by their pupil – she lost every game – the nieces curbed their habitual aggressiveness, taking their job to heart. Although convinced that their attitude arose only from self interest, Kham-Phiou was grateful to them for having created an atmosphere favourable for a positive relationship. To further improve the relationship, she decided to follow their example and chew betel.

In Lao tradition, a betel chew is composed of a betel leaf *(baeuy phou[1])* brushed with lime, and then folded once. Onto this are placed a piece of bark of *peuak had[2]*, a piece of *sisiaet[3]* bark, a piece of areca nut *(mak[4])*, and sometimes cloves *(kan phou[5])*, and the whole folded in a small package. Once the betel is chewed, it is spat out in the form of a red juice into a spittoon *(ngiaeng[6])* and the chewer cleans the teeth with tobacco rolled in the shape of a small ball before applying lip balm.

Chewing betel was only adopted by adults or by adolescents after marriage. The practice of chewing betel despite its reputation of strengthening teeth, has the disadvantage of reddening the saliva while chewing. As a result practitioners have to spit regularly into spittoons placed at their sides.

Silk and gold embroidered Phra Bot.

Souvanna Phouma loathed the practice and was appalled when he saw his wife with *phai tong* cards in her hand, calmly chewing betel like her neighbours. When they were alone in their room he asked her to refrain from the practice in future.

Apart from learning *phai tong*, Kham-Phiou, at her husband's request, began making little bags out of jute cloth to contain the mining samples to be sent to France. She enjoyed this work and she carried it out in her room with a degree of artistry which justified her husband's compliments. In fact, she also mastered the art of *pak ding[7]*, the royal embroidery which is a hand-stitched technique using gold or silver threads, pearls and spangles and is traditionally used as an ornament for religious purposes such as ceremonial fans *(khan talabat[8])*, triangular or rectangular cushions *(mone thao[9])*, votive offerings representing the Buddha *(phra bot)*, Court or military garments and accessories. The patterns are inspired by the friezes and motifs of traditional wood carvings.

"Very good, very good indeed," he commented.

Moreover, she also surprised him by her talents in making her own corsages and skirts.

"You know, in France everything that is hand-sewn is very expensive. There you would save a lot of money."

"Here it is the opposite," she replied, "machine-stitched garments are more expensive, but they are preferred."

Then, in a different tone, he asked her point-blank:

"Do you know how to darn socks?"

"NO." she replied.

She knew how to sew, to embroider to weave, to make flower arrangements for festivals at the temple, but not to darn socks – something she had never learned nor had had any need to learn.

"I shall teach you to darn socks," he told her.

Intrigued she asked him how he could have acquired such a housewifely skill – surely a job reserved for women.

"I learned in France," he replied. "While studying there I had to learn to shop, to cook, to do housework, to sew on buttons and to darn socks."

On the fifteenth day of the waxing and waning moon, the enlarged family always gathered around Princess Sa-Ngiem Kham and her husband, Prince Souvannarath, who was always present on these occasions, for lunch at Hong Taeuy. As usual the men dined in the reception hall in Western style, while the women were in the private quarters seated on mats around a large circular tray.

In the afternoon, men and women played *phai tong* in their respective areas. It was on one of these occasions that Kham-Phiou won for the first time – an apotheosis in Souvanna Phouma's eyes.

"You must be intelligent," he rejoiced, "those who do not know how to play *phai tong* have no brains."[10]

Souvanna Phouma enjoyed listening to his wife reading old tales. One evening she asked him which story he would like her to read. Slightly maliciously he suggested the story of a sparrow couple from "500 lives of the Buddha". The couple had just had an adorable fledgeling, who was still unable to fly, when a fire broke out in the forest where they lived. Both its parents swore they would not let him die alone. But, when the flames got close, the male flew off, completely abandoning his family.

"But that's not true," exclaimed Souvanna Phouma, "it was the female bird who flew away."

"It IS true, it WAS the male who flew away," interrupted Kham-Phiou, "the mother bird remained with her child."

"In my opinion it was the male who remained,' reiterated Souvanna Phouma.

"Look, read what is written," retorted Kham-Phiou very indignantly, holding out the manuscript so her husband could read it for himself.

He could no longer stop himself from bursting out laughing.

"Oh you are teasing me again," said Kham-Phiou crossly. Then seeing how ridiculous the situation was, she also laughed with her husband.

Another day, Souvanna Phouma teased her by showing her a photo of himself in France walking arm in arm with a young girl. Noting their proximity, Kham-Phiou immediately recalled many cases of

French officers and bureaucrats who having married Laotian wives while posted in Laos, abandoned them once their tour of duty was over, and returned to France and their French wives.

Her throat tightened as she asked: "Is that your wife?"

"No. Just a friend."

"How can she be just a friend, holding your arm like that?"

Amused by her naiveté, he reassured her that this was indeed the case and that in France ordinary friends showed affection by walking arm in arm without this signifying any other closer relationship. And to illustrate and explain French manners more clearly, he demonstrated the various ways French people greeted each other: for example, the handshake, the hug and kissing a lady's hand. Kham-Phiou had seen French people in Luang Prabang shaking hands, but hugging made her blush, while having her hand kissed tickled and made her laugh till her tears came.

The closeness and understanding between the young couple grew day by day. The threatening family atmosphere seemed to have been neutralised. Kham-Phiou now almost always accompanied Souvanna Phouma on his trips into the countryside, finding the same pleasure in these trips as on the first occasion.

One day, Souvanna Phouma suspected that his wife was pregnant. This thrilled him beyond words. The idea that Kham-Phiou might be carrying his child altered his view of her. The importance she had already gained in his eyes now greatly exceeded his respect for the etiquette governing their daily life. From now on a simplified style of behaviour deepened their relationship.

The day after his return from one of the prospecting expeditions, Kham-Phiou wearying of making bags for pebbles, dared to question her husband.

"Well, O trader in pebbles, where is all this getting us?"[11] she sighed.

"Believe me," he answered. "You will see. The day this trader in pebbles finds a mine, let me tell you, we shall be rich beyond our dreams, and for generations to come."[12]

A doubting Kham-Phiou could not grasp how the sale of little pebbles could ever lead to such fortune.

The prospect of having a child led Souvanna Phouma to show an interest in Ekarath, the youngest of his elder sister's children. In the late afternoon, when the inhabitants of the Hong Taeuy were gathered on the veranda, he liked to carry the child in his arms, imitating his babbling and addressing him in French. One day after playing with the child for some time, he set him on Kham-Phiou's knees, saying jokingly:

"You must start getting used to this: soon it will be our child's turn."

Contrary to his expectations, that remark deeply upset the family. Instead of the sound of cheerful conversation and laughing children, a heavy silence fell over the veranda like lead. What had seemed to be an extinct volcano threatened to explode again. Kham-Phiou felt overwhelmed with fear.

Chapter 9

Greatness and Jealousy

Since his marriage Souvanna Phouma had not seen the king. His Majesty Sisavang Vong[1] granted him an audience at the Royal Palace. He went there accompanied by his half-brother and brother-in-law, Prince Souvannarath.

Upon his return to Hong Taeuy, he hastened to inform Kham-Phiou of the great honour which the king had paid him:

"It was extraordinary: His Majesty took off his hat to shake my hand but did not do the same to my elder brother."

Souvanna Phouma himself thought this gesture was in recognition of his brilliant academic record in his engineering studies in public works and later electricity in Paris and Grenoble between 1925 and 1929 which had made him the first Laotian engineer.

At the same time this signal and unusual honour gave him hope that he might eventually fulfil his childhood ambition of carrying out some important task for his country.

As always Kham-Phiou listened attentively to Souvanna Phouma's statements, but due to her youth and inexperience it took some time before she was able to realise the importance of the signal honour the king had bestowed on her husband.

More self assured than ever, Souvanna Phouma painted a picture of the virtues of the ancient rulers of the Kingdom of the Million Elephants and of the White Parasol and finished by a severe critique of the depraved morals of certain of his near relatives who misbehaved with maids and even the ladies-in-waiting of their wives.

Usually after finishing her housework in her own room, Kham-Phiou would go to give a helping hand to her sister-in-law. One day while she was peeling vegetables in the kitchen, her husband indicated she had no role to play in that place, remarking "we do have a cook to do such things."

Kham-Phiou, highly mortified in front of Princess Sa-Ngiem Kham, whom she knew it was her duty to help, abandoned her task. She went back into the house, puzzled and unable to understand her husband's motives.

Later, during the weekly visit from her mother, Souvanna Phouma caught his mother-in-law addressing her as 'little one' *(noy²)* – the affectionate term used by all Laotian mothers to their children. The use of this word offended him and he openly rebuked his mother-in-law:

"Kham-Phiou is, of course, your daughter but she is now my wife and you should respect her married status as my wife by addressing her as 'Mom Kham-Phiou'."

Such a remark from her son-in-law completely stunned Nang Phya Kham-Douang. Unable to find words in reply, she left and never again entered the Mansion. As a consequence Kham-Phiou had to increase her visits to her mother's quarter, which was certainly no problem for her, but which definitely annoyed Souvanna Phouma.

His conscious insistence on his wife being always accorded the honorific *'kham'* - a prefix reserved for the nobility and the aristocracy led him to rebuke Princess Sa-Ngiem Kham with a similar comment.

"Why do you only call my wife 'Phiou'? Her name is 'Kham-Phiou', accenting the 'Kham'. Even I address her as Kham-Phiou. As my wife she is now 'Mom Kham-Phiou'. She is in any case the granddaughter of Tiao Phanya Na Neua and the daughter of Tiao Phanya Luang Mun Na, the first President when alive of the Court of Appeal and a first cousin of *thou nyaeuy* Kommasang³."

Momentarily taken aback by her brother's attack, the exasperated princess took a little while to recover her self-possession. Conscious of her status as the Elder Sister, she made gestures of appeasement but slowly and clearly stated:

"Well, I address her as 'Phiou' and that should be quite good enough."[4]

Obtaining no concession from his sister, Souvanna Phouma left in a bad temper, not realising that his own ill-advised intervention led to his sister conceiving an even greater dislike of Kham-Phiou, casting her in the role of an ambitious and hypocritical intruder in the family and considering Souvanna Phouma as her innocent dupe whom she was leading by the nose.

Chapter 10

The Tragedy

The final expedition of Souvanna Phouma in search of minerals was into a heavily forested hilly area, only accessible on horseback. For this reason Kham-Phiou did not accompany her husband.

The memory of the bad treatment she had suffered each time he went away would have rightly disturbed her, if it were not for her husband's solemn sworn promise to be back quickly. However, on the third day after his departure her fears were justified. Opening the door of her bedroom in the early morning, she found the nieces lying in the private hall. One of them even blocked the door, forcing Kham-Phiou to step ultra cautiously around the edge of the room to avoid stepping on her. But suddenly a strident cry startled her and awoke the whole household.

"She stepped over me, she stepped over me[1]!" yelled the niece and getting up in tears she yelled louder, pointing at the 'guilty party'.

Stunned by this total invention, Kham-Phiou merely looked at the girl and went silently down the stairs to the bathroom. On her return an unpleasant surprise awaited her: Princess Sa-Ngiem Kham sent for her and admonished her severely. Bewildered but with her conscience clear, Kham-Phiou asked:

"Do you really believe me capable of such behaviour?"

"How dare you answer me back?" shouted the furious princess. "Just because my brother spoils you, you think you are superior and entitled to do what you like here. It has become total anarchy in this house!"

Kham-Phiou said no more. Shocked that her sister-in-law believed the allegations of her niece and shocked by the vehemence of this speech, she felt feverish. Retiring to her room for the rest of that day, she did not join the family for lunch. By the afternoon her temperature had risen so much that she could not move at all.

Two days later when she had not been seen outside her bedroom, a servant was sent to check and reported that she had a high fever, was losing blood and was delirious. Panic stricken, her sister-in-law sent for Kham-Phiou's paternal grandfather, Kham-Pheng Tiao Phanya Na Neua, the man whom Souvanna Phouma had asked for permission to marry Kham-Phiou, who was living in the same quarter of Vat That. Tiao Phanya Na Neua immediately had Kham-Phiou carried to his own house to treat her with medicinal herbs and sent a messenger in haste to find Souvanna Phouma.

As soon as he got the news, Souvanna Phouma set off for Luang Prabang at a gallop through the night, escaping by miracle a tiger attack. Reaching his wife's bedside, he watched over her till daybreak when, replaced by Kham-Phaeng, a younger sister of Kham-Phiou, he went to Hong Taeuy to bathe and change his clothes and to snatch a few hours rest before returning to her side, remaining there night and day until she recovered a little.

Some days later, thanks to the care of her grandfather, she had somewhat improved and could take some rice porridge which gradually gave her back her strength.

Greatly relieved but deeply affected, Souvanna Phouma said to her: "I know what made you so ill, it was them."

Together they wept over their fate, the loss after only a month's pregnancy of what would have been their child.

Following this most painful period, Souvanna Phouma ceased almost all communication with his family members and their entourage. For their part the nieces adopted a low profile and, against all odds, Princess Sa-Ngiem Kham, smitten with remorse, showed great and sincere kindness to Kham-Phiou.

Some weeks later, when Kham-Phiou was fully recovered, Souvanna Phouma told her of his intention to join the French administration as an engineer in the Department of Public Works in Vientiane, the administrative capital. This idea had been suggested by his elder brother, Prince Phetsarath. To Souvanna Phouma it seemed to be the best solution for their future.

Prince Phetsarath, the second son of Viceroy Bounkhong, of the Front Lineage, was born in 1890, three years before the French protectorate over the Kingdom of Luang Prabang. After a primary apprenticeship in French from 1896 to 1904, he pursued secondary studies at Lycée Chasseloup-Laubat in Saigon and then at Lycée Montaigne and Lycée Saint-Louis in Paris. His studies ended at the École Coloniale in 1913.

On his return to Laos in 1914, he was recruited by the Royal Treasury in Luang Prabang. Spotted by Claude Léon Garnier, the Senior French Resident of Laos, he was hired by the latter's secretariat in 1915. In this capacity, he accompanied him on his provincial inspections and gained a reputation throughout the country.

From then on, his rise in the French colonial administration continued to progress: in 1919 he was promoted to Director of the Bureau of Indigenous Affairs and established the School of Law and Administration in Vientiane. In the same year, the Governor General of Indochina appointed him Indigenous Inspector of Political and Administrative Affairs of Laos.

In this position he established an Indigenous Consultative Assembly comprising all the heads of provinces and districts of Laos. In the early 1930s, in addition to his position as Indigenous Inspector, he was appointed head of the Lao Buddhist Council. In this way he was able to reorganise the clergy and create Pali schools in the country.

Given the high administrative position of Phetsarath and his rank in the family line, Kham-Phiou could not contradict her husband but she dreaded being so far from her mother particularly as communications between Luang Prabang and Vientiane, principally by water, were very slow.

Chapter 11

Souvanna Phouma
moves to Vientiane

Souvanna Phouma's move to Vientiane, while intended to make married life tolerable for Kham-Phiou, posed two major problems: the first was that his salary would be only a twentieth of what he had received from the French mining company and, to make matters worse, would only be paid at the end of the month.

The second problem was accommodation: without any financial means he would be unable to rent a property and would have to depend on the hospitality of his elder brother Prince Phetsarath and his wife, 'Princess-One-Eye'.

The couple had financed Souvanna Phouma's extensive studies from 1915 to 1928 in Hanoi and France and were expecting to be repaid by his marriage to one of their daughters. In these circumstances it was impossible for Souvanna Phouma to bring his wife to live with them. Her position in that household would be exactly the same as in Luang Prabang – in fact probably even worse as his sister- in-law was famous for her spitefulness and vulgarity.

Souvanna Phouma thought it wise not to impart these problems to Kham-Phiou, merely telling her he would need to go in advance to find suitable accommodation and take up his duties as Chief Executive of the Public Works Department.

So one morning in July 1931 at the start of the rainy season, the couple bade each other good bye at the Messageries Maritimes Port of Tha Heua Me in the Hong Taeuy Quarter. Good manners forbade any show of emotion or embraces. Only the tears in the eyes of Kham-Phiou betrayed her emotion as she stood holding a large packet of cigarettes, lovingly prepared with her own hands, enclosed in a banana leaf. For his part, Souvanna Phouma took off the sapphire ring he always wore, a family heirloom, and slid it on to Kham-Phiou's finger.

"I will write regularly," he promised.

"I will never fail to reply," she answered, lowering her eyes to hide her tears, "and to send you cigarettes."

"Remain at the Mansion," he ordered, "it is a family property belonging to me and my brothers and sisters. As my wife it is your right to live in my room even when I am away. I have told my sister you will live there. Get your things together ready to join me as soon as you receive word from me by letter."

Kham-Phiou agreed, hardly able to hear her husband's words. Her mind was invaded by a thousand thoughts, unhappy memories mixed with speculations about a future at present shrouded in mist. When she realised the boat, already in the centre of the river, had begun its voyage, her tears fell like rain.

Obeying the wishes of Souvanna Phouma, she resigned herself to remaining at the Mansion, waiting every day for news of her husband. A month later, Princess Sa-Ngiem Kham called her.

"I have a little cake for you," she said. "Come here," and dipping her hand into her bag she drew out an envelope.

Kham-Phiou immediately understood that it was the long-awaited letter. In his letter Souvanna Phouma described his trouble-free journey and his temporary lodging with his elder brother, his frustration at the unforeseen slow bureaucracy which was delaying his taking up his post even though this should be sorted out in the near future. He adjured her to stay at the Mansion and to be ready to catch the boat. He finished by saying how much he missed her and how much he hoped they would be together again soon.

Unlike Souvanna Phouma's elder sister who now treated her with consideration and kindness, the nieces continued their campaign of spitefulness and made her life as difficult and unpleasant as they could and Kham-Phiou longed to leave the Mansion.

At the end of August, her mother's illness gave her a good excuse to stay in her maternal home instead. She wrote to her husband to inform him and enclosed a big packet of hand-rolled cigarettes she had made for him. Her letter only reached him at the end of September.

Souvanna Phouma was upset that she had gone to her mother's house and fearing his mother-in-law was trying to separate them and keep her daughter, he ordered Kham-Phiou to catch the next boat to Vientiane which would be in November. At the same time he told his elder brother and sister-in-law that he was sending for his wife.

Hardly surprisingly, his sister-in-law was furious at this disruption of their plans and reproached him bitterly. However, her furious reaction did not stop at reproaches: she immediately bribed the postman to intercept any of Kham-Phiou's letters to Souvanna Phouma and deliver them to her instead of him. She followed this action by instructing a female friend who was taking the boat to Luang Prabang to warn Kham-Phiou's mother to keep her daughter at home.

"If by any chance," her message ran, 'your daughter comes to Vientiane to join her husband, I shall immediately throw her out of the house. If however she is willing to suffer being beaten with rattan and canes, then let her come. But on her head be it and at her own peril!'

Kham-Phiou's mother's pride was deeply wounded by this insulting message and she wrote back saying she preferred a thousand times to ensure her daughter spent the whole of the year worshipping and doing good works in the temples of Luang Prabang rather than send her to spend her time playing *phai tong* and listening to malicious gossip and slanders in Vientiane.

A violent postal war of words between the two lasted until 1932.

To emphasise her independence from her son-in-law, Kham-Phiou's mother returned the 20 piastres a month that he had paid her as agreed in the marriage contract. She informed her daughter that under no circumstances should she join her husband in Vientiane. Kham-Phiou wrote to her husband telling him of all these sad and serious events which now prevented her leaving Luang Prabang.

Souvanna Phouma, ignorant of his sister-in-law's suppression of letters from Kham-Phiou, cycled to the pier every month to meet the boat from Luang Prabang, but there was neither his wife nor any letter from her. He immediately jumped to the conclusion that this was due to his mother-in-law, whose wish to cause a break with him had already been signalled by the return of the 20 piastres. He believed it would have required all her authority as a mother to persuade Kham-Phiou to agree to this. But nevertheless, in order to be sure, he sent a letter to Kham-Phiou by the December boat to ask why she had not come to Vientiane when he asked.

Kham-Phiou was stupefied to receive this reply, explaining once again her position and begging him to come himself and fetch her. This in her eyes was now the only solution to the impasse in which she found herself.

The reply from Souvanna Phouma, who, of course, had never received her letter and knew nothing of his sister-in-law's threats, stunned and shook her, it was an ultimatum designed to force her to choose between her mother and him. He said he would only wait another two months for her to join him.

"If you do not come within this time," he warned her, "I shall be free to take another wife, not one of my nieces but a non-blood relative. You will see, despite what your mother thinks, that I shall never marry a blood relative."

Kham-Phiou knew from experience that her husband spoke the truth. He was a man of his word. She consulted her closest friend, Onesy, the girl whose stall she had shared when she first met Souvanna Phouma at the new year celebrations. Onesy was definite.

"He is your husband," she said, "he loves you and you love him. You should go to him: there is no reason to abandon him to another wife."

Convinced by the logic of the reasoning, Kham-Phiou for the first time dared to disobey her mother. She secretly assembled her luggage and confided it to her friend. Early in the morning of the boat's departure, helped by Onesy, she took her luggage down to the boat and prepared to embark. But the boat captain refused to let her board. He told her:

"Your mother came to me in tears and pleaded with me not to take you."

Shattered by this unforeseeable refusal, Kham-Phiou collapsed shaking and in tears, realising at this moment that she had now lost forever her beloved husband.

"Why, oh why, would you not come and fetch me?" she sobbed. Through her tears she saw the boat cast off, set sail towards the centre of the river and then make its way downstream. The last time she had watched it sail away it had carried her husband, himself full of confidence, leaving his desperate wife on the bank. At this moment, as if watching a film, she recalled all her unhappiness and sufferings and a fierce and overwhelming desire to die swept over her.

Onesy held her tight, trying in vain to think of some way to console her, and frightened at her own helplessness in the face of this immense tragedy for which they were totally unprepared.

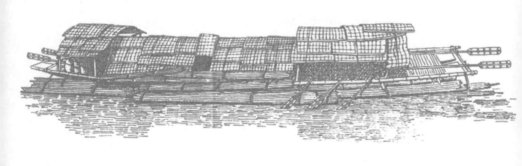

Chapter 12

Of long divergent destinies

Kham-Phiou and her friend were completely crushed. They made their way back to Kham-Phiou's mother's house, their heads bowed. Onesy helped her friend carry her bag up to the veranda and then left without speaking. Lying in a state of collapse over her bag, the symbol now of her lost hopes, Kham-Phiou offered no resistance to her mother's expected fury. But strangely, Nang Phya Kham-Douang made no reproach or even comment. Instead she soothed her daughter gently as if she were still a child.

As to Souvanna Phouma he was installed as Head of the departmental section of architecture and public buildings of the Public Works Department in Vientiane. At the same time he was also made Director of the Water and Electricity Works. It was in this capacity that in 1932 he oversaw the provision of running water in Vientiane.

He did not fulfil his threat to Kham-Phiou to remarry within two months. It was only ten months later that he married an Eurasian girl, the daughter of a French father and Lao mother from Xieng Khouang province. This decision, taken after careful consideration, had two advantages from Souvanna Phouma's view. It finally put paid to the lasting hopes of his elder relatives that he would choose a wife from among their daughters and it also demonstrated to his mother-in-law that even when separated from Kham-Phiou he had not married a close female relative. The latter would have to admit that her son-in-law had kept his word not to marry a person of the nobility. Besides, this second marriage gave him an entrée to the French administration, assisting his rise in his new career. The couple had four children.

Nang Phya Kham-Phiou with husband Phya Kham-Ouane, sister Kham-Pin and adopted brother Thid Onekaeo.

Knowing that Kham-Phiou was now free to remarry, several young men from good families in Luang Prabang wished to court her. But her mother discouraged all approaches. However, when one of her distant nephews, Kham-Ouane, who had trained at the School of Law and Administration in Vientiane made an approach she agreed immediately. Kham-Ouane at this time held the post of Deputy Mayor of Bountay, in Phongsaly Province, with particular responsibility as Coordinator for liaison with the French military authorities[1]. Kham-Phiou herself had no memory of this cousin, some twelve years older than her.

Kham-Ouane held the title of Phya Ratana Koumphon. His father Kham-Peng, Tiao Phanya Luang Muang Phaen, Governor of Luang Namtha Province, was a direct descendant in the fourth generation of the famous Tiao Phanya Luang Muang Saen Khaeo Khao, known as the 'Lord-with-White-Teeth'[2], who had been the first owner of the Downstream Mansion during the reign of King Anourouth at the end of the eighteenth and beginning of the nineteenth century.

Another property included a mansion in Ban Pak Khan where Kham-Ouane grew up. It was built on the land at the very end of the peninsula, overlooking both the Mekong and Nam Khan rivers. The family temple of Vat Pak Khan[3] was accessible from the mansion by a small path. The property stayed within Kham-Ouane's family until the early 1940's, when the French administration decided to enlarge the road and to build the Customs House. Kham-Ouane's family was thus expropriated and relocated downstream in Vat Sop Quarter.

The wedding of Kham-Phiou and Kham-Ouane – more prestigious than the first one and this time consolidating her family status and connections in the eyes of Nang Phya Kham-Douang – was celebrated in 1935. It took place under the auspices of Prince Kindavong, the Governor of the Province of Phongsaly. On his father's side, he was a half-brother of Souvanna Phouma and on his mother's side, a third cousin to Kham-Ouane and a second cousin to Kham-Phiou. He was also very close to the latter, whom he had known since her childhood, when he was living with her parents in Vientiane to continue his studies at the School of Law and Administration.

The following year, Nang Phya Kham-Douang died. Kham-Phiou, confined to bed by a miscarriage in Bountay, was sadly unable to be present at her mother's funeral services. Following these tragic events the house at Sieng Mouane, now devoid of family members was rented out to relatives.

Kham-Phiou bore her husband two children, the first a boy was born in 1937. The night before his birth Kham-Phiou dreamed that her father, who had died in 1925 had come to her house carrying his belongings. She installed him as was proper near the altar of the Buddha, in the room overlooking the front veranda. Having slept there for one night he left with his belongings. As a result of this dream Kham-Phiou gave her son the name of Kham-Phoui in remembrance of his maternal grandfather Tiao Phanya Luang Mun Na.

According to the customs of noble and aristocratic families the eldest children[4] got all the attention and so it had been in Kham-Phiou's family. Her elder brother Kham-Phay who was studying medicine in

Phya Kham-Ouane, during an official tour in Phongsaly Province. In the foreground, Lu and Tai Dam women wearing traditional clothes.

Hanoi was the object of all his mother's attention, while Kham-Phiou as eldest daughter had had all her father's attention. On her father's death when she was twelve she played her part in all household affairs and looked after her younger brother and sisters like a second mother, but this did not prevent her from missing her beloved father bitterly and suffering deeply at his death.

Her second child was a girl born in Bountay two years later. The child's father gave her the name of Thong-Samouth ('Gold of the Oceans') in memory of Nong Samouth, the great lake where his revered ancestor Tiao Phanya Luang Muang Saen, from whom he had inherited his property, held annual regattas. The lake was sold later by Kham-Peng's younger sister, aunt Kham-Fong, who was married to the Governor of Pak Beng Province, in order to build a temple in Pak Beng. This second birth gave boundless joy. A small dog named Bak Kit was adopted at the same time and grew up alongside the child. Despite his long absences due to his work, he pampered his little girl as much as possible. Every Sunday, to the great indignation of Kham-Phiou, he brought her a little present, because she was born on a Sunday.

At the time, the province of Phongsaly to which the district of Bountay belonged, was still strongly marked by its links with the ancient kingdom of Sipsong Panna. The latter, located on the borders of North Laos and the Chinese province of Yunnan, formed a vassal kingdom of the Chinese Empire until the early 19th century, when it was the object of strategic stakes on both sides, resulting in its partition between China and Laos. The majority population of Sipsong Panna is the Lu ethnic group, close cousin of the Lao. Although subject to the vagaries of external conflict, the Lu continued to maintain their kinship ties with other northern Tai groups of the princely states of Luang Prabang, Chiang Mai in Lan Na and Kengtung in the Shan States. Each year, the full moon of the twelfth month of the Buddhist calendar is still the occasion of a great pilgrimage of the Lu from all over the region to That Xieng Tung, the sacred stupa of the city of Muang Sing, located in the province of Luang Namtha.

Phya Kham-Ouane lived with his family in a house belonging to the French administration that included a fireplace, essential during the cold winters of this region located on the last the foothills of the Himalayas. In addition, the architecture of Phongsaly, typical of the Yunnan style, consisted of brick constructions covered with raised roofs.

Because of this mountainous typography, the most common means of transport was the horse. Nang Kham-Phiou, accompanied by her attendant, used to ride sidesaddle. A suite of grooms, porters, and servants accompanied her on each of her journeys. When the trip was longer, a sedan chair *(ham⁵)* took over. There were eight bearers, taking turns of four at a time.

During the early years of their childhood in Bountay, and despite the global conflict that affected the entire region, Kham-Phoui and Thong-Samouth enjoyed a serene environment favoured by a generous nature. They were surrounded by wild animals that the peasants brought as gifts to their father. The latter had also put them in the saddle from an early age, and they had become accomplished riders. Sometimes they were given permission to swim with their nanny in the nearby Nam Laeng stream, and each time they came back in awe when they saw that the Lu women who were also bathing, would dip a basin in the stream and bring out an impressive amount of fish.

The household had a small farm yard. Knowing the religious disposition of their mistress, the servants took a malicious pleasure in teasing her when they were about to cook the meals: "Madame, which chicken do you prefer that we cook, the black one or the red one?" Invariably Nang Kham-Phiou responded each time with a horrified gesture: "I do not want to know anything about it!"

Phya Kham-Ouane's family was close to that of Captain Jehan Delpech de Frayssinet. He had been based in the Phongsaly area since the early 1940s as a captain, then lieutenant-colonel of aviation. Their daughters, who were about the same age, shared their games. When they travelled to Vientiane aboard the seaplane, he often lifted Thong-Samouth up to the porthole to admire the incessant swooping of the swallows who came and went in the shelter of the steep cliffs overlooking the Mekong River.

A climate of great confusion affected the fate of people living in the heart of the conflict zones. One day, Nang Saeng, the daughter of Tiao Maha Phom, a son of the 43rd ruler of Sipsong Panna[6], when visiting relatives in Phongsaly, met Thid One Kaeo, the adopted brother of Phya Kham-Ouane. This young man, although not himself from a prominent family, was acceptable as a son-in-law to Nang Saeng's family, due to his relationship with the family of Phya Kham-Ouane. After her marriage, Nang Saeng moved from the princely mansion where she grew up near Chiang Hung, the capital city of Sipsong Panna to Bountay. Among her suite that accompanied her was Nang Kham-Lu ('Gold', 'Lu') who a few years later, returned in Sipsong Panna to marry. On her return, people renamed her 'Nang Kham-Lao' ('Gold', 'Lao'). Sadly, the marriage between Thid One Kaeo and Nang Saeng did not prosper. It turned out that the husband was not worthy of her. A new opportunity for marriage came when, with the advancing Chinese troops of the Kuomintang in Northern Laos, Nang Saeng met a young Chinese officer with whom she went to live in Taiwan.

Although culturally close, the Lu are distinguished from other Tai groups by ritual practices of their own. Thus, one day when Thong-Samouth, who had been in poor health from birth, was seized with an attack of violent fever that had greatly weakened her, a shaman

(mo yao⁷) was called up. The latter began his consultation and discovered the reason for this pain: the child had come into the world in secret, without the permission of her celestial parents. The *mo yao* then undertook a ritual that lasted a whole week, consisting of chantings to call the souls in order to help the patient to climb

Nang Phya Kham-Phiou and her two children.

the tree linking terrestrial beings to celestial beings. At each stage, a chicken or pork was sacrificed. The progression on the tree was very slow and exhausting. Nevertheless, the goal was reached and the child fully recovered.

In 1940 Souvanna Phouma was placed in charge of constructing the sector of the proposed National Highway 13 between Vientiane and Phou Khoun. The following year he was promoted to Chief Engineer of the Luang Prabang Public Works for a period of three years and was overjoyed to be able to return to the city of his birth. He

Nang Phya Kham-Phiou and daughter Thong-Samouth.

was entitled to an official residence, a colonial villa on the bank of the Mekong in the same area as Hong Taeuy.

During 1942 Kham-Phiou had occasion to visit Luang Prabang with her two children and stayed with her elder brother, now Dr Kham-Phay who on his return from Hanoi had settled in the Fak Phou Quarter (called 'the other side of the mountain') on the south side of the city, close to the provincial hospital of the time.

One day when she was taking her children out in a cycle rickshaw along the main road which led to the end of the peninsula, a cyclist stopped in front of her and imperiously commanded the driver to halt.

It was Souvanna Phouma. It was the first time they met since their separation. White to the gills, his throat tight with emotion, he stammered:

"Kham-Phiou, Kham-Phiou! What beautiful children you have!"

Stupefied and on the verge of tears, Kham-Phiou could only tell the driver to drive on.

"Where are you staying?" demanded Souvanna Phouma insistently.

The driver was continuing the journey, as she managed to just gasp, "at my brother's."

Reaching her destination she locked herself in her room and burst into tears. In a panic, her children stood on either side of her and, feverishly patted her while asking: "Mother why are you crying, who is scolding you?"[8], which only made her cry harder.

Souvanna Phouma appeared at nightfall and his arrival made things no better. Despite her brother's insistence, she neither could nor would leave her bedroom. What good could it do? The reappearance of the man she loved seemed a trap, like a treasure close by but unreachable. He had remarried. She had remarried. They both had children. All discussion seemed pointless.

The fastest way to get from Luang Prabang to Bountay was to sail on the Mekong River to Pak Ou, then go up the Nam Ou River to Hat Sa and Muang Khoua, before continuing on horseback to Phongsaly province. However, the Nam Ou being impassable during the dry season (from November to April), it was necessary to take a second river road up the Mekong River to Pak Beng, then from there travel by a route that ran past Muang Houn, a postal station to the south of Phongsaly Province, and finally Bountay and Phongsaly.

It was during the dry season that Kham-Phiou and her children on their way back to Bountay from Luang Prabang stayed overnight in Muang Houn. As night fell the boy complained of stomach pains. Informed by telegram, his father rode at a gallop towards Muang Houn but he could not arrive in time. The boy died during the night. The funeral was held in Bountay in the presence of Prince Kindavong.

His parents loved each other but in different ways. To Kham-Phiou her husband was like a big brother while he loved her passionately. But both parents adored their children and this death was an unspeakable sorrow to both of them.

A sudden appendicitis was the probable cause of the child's death. The owners of the house where Kham-Phiou and her children stayed overnight attributed his death to the anger of the spirit of the house which resented his having touched objects on the altars of the ancestors.

For her part, Kham-Phiou remembered the dream she had of her father on the eve of giving birth to her son. He had been carrying his belongings and had only stayed one night. This signified that her child would not live long. Following this thought she wondered whether her son would not have died if she had not given him her father's name. She kept seeing in her mind her son's lovable nature, his face with its black curly hair so like her own.

Having suffered two miscarriages and lost little Kham-Phoui, she began to doubt her ability to give life and to raise children.

The following year, Kham-Phiou returned to Luang Prabang with her daughter as the relatives who rented her house had fled to Chiang Saen, where many Luang Prabang people had connections, on the other bank of the Mekong River in Northern Thailand, as a consequence of their families rallying to the beginnings of Lao independence movements. One of those movements would later be the Lao Issara created in 1945 with its members exiled in Bangkok.

But regional events and the vagaries of travel prevented Kham-Phiou and her daughter from returning to Bountay.

When, following the Japanese coup in March 1945, Kham-Ouane joined the Free French Forces in Calcutta via Simao and Kunming, he left the care of the house in Bountay, as well as Bak Kit, Thong-Samouth's dog, to a trusted man, a trader. In a telegram to his wife, he asked her to go and get these things from Muang Khoua district. However, when the latter went there she found that there was not much left. All their precious effects, including the silverware, had disappeared. She returned to Luang Prabang with just a few items and Bak Kit, only after paying the cost of the dog's food for which the merchant had also claimed payment.

Chapter 13

Laos in the turmoil of wars

After his three-year posting in Luang Prabang, Prince Souvanna Phouma attained the peak of his career as an engineer when he was appointed Head of the Public Works Department in Vientiane and in 1944 he and his family re-established themselves in the administrative capital of Laos.

On the 13th May 1946 the Franco-Lao troops of Xieng Khouang reconquered Luang Prabang, where the king had been re-crowned on the 23rd April 1946. There the king declared the attachment of his kingdom to France. Among these troops was Phya Kham-Ouane Ratana Koumphon, the husband of Kham-Phiou, who was appointed both Mayor and Police Commissioner of the royal capital. He indeed was in perfect continuity with his ancestor, Tiao Phanya Luang Muang Saen Khaeo Khao, truly loyal to the Great Royal Lineage and carried out these functions faithfully.

Upon his arrival in Luang Prabang by seaplane, among all the people who had assembled on the banks of the Mekong River at Tha Heua Me, he saw his mother weeping before him. Kham-Mao, her younger son who was a civil servant in Luang Prabang had been denounced by the people and imprisoned by the French as a collaborator. Without taking the time to change, Kham-Ouane immediately went to the Royal Palace to request an audience with the king. He said: "Sire, of all my relatives, I only have this young brother left. I implore your leniency". King Sisavang Vong, who had retained the prerogatives for internal affairs, greatly appreciated Phya Kham-Ouane personally, and had the conviction lifted. But his cousin Tiao Syhanath, the younger brother of Prince Kindavong, who was also in the same situation, had not the same luck since his brother was at that time still stationed in France and did not have time to come to Luang Prabang to ask for the grace of his brother. He was shot. This period of settlings of accounts also saw the lynching of the former Governor of Xieng Khouang Province, Phanya Kham-Lek, who had been delivered to the Hmong population by the French.

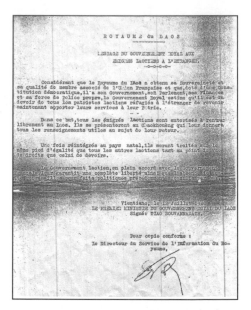

Lao royal government's message to Lao emigrants allowing them to return home and guaranteeing them the same rights as other Laotians (12 July 1948).

At the same time, in a spirit of appeasement and national reconciliation, the king pardoned the various parties, including those who had threatened him and the Royal family and stolen the Royal Treasure[1]. Supporters of the Lao Issara movement were also allowed to return to Laos and recover their property that had been seized. Thus life resumed its course in Luang Prabang, and in particular in Ban Sieng Mouane where all the factions in the family and relatives, irrespective of which party they belonged to, met and mingled with each other again as before.

Under his administration of the city, Kham-Ouane with other civil servants organised small sketches intended to enliven the population of Luang Prabang and to collect money for charities during these post-war times.

In May 1947, the King of Luang Prabang became the sovereign of a new state: a unified Laos, monarchic and parliamentary by its constitution. To mark the event, His Majesty decided to celebrate the Great Feast of the twelfth month that closed the annual cycle of

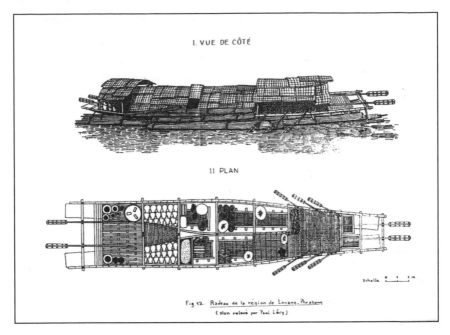

I. VUE DE CÔTÉ

II PLAN

Echelle

Fig. 12. Radeau de la région de Louang-Phrabang
(plan relevé par Paul Lévy)

Heua mo.

festivals, not in Luang Prabang, but in Vientiane, the royal capital of his ancestor Setthathirath, in the sixteenth century.

For the occasion, an important procession of several *heua mo*[2] carrying the high officials and their families, the Royal guard, the Royal Ramayana troop *(phra lak phra lam*[3]*)* along with the Royal dancers *(nang kaeo*[4]*)* and the Royal puppet troop *(i pok*[5]*)*[v] – something totally unknown to the population in Vientiane at that time and the staff of the Palace, made the long journey downstream lasting several days and nights.

Another *heua mo* was specially assigned for the transport of the ritual objects and dishes, and the ceremonial outfits and weapons.

Unlike the other members of the procession sharing several of the *heua mo*, Kham-Ouane, who was responsible for the safety of the royal objects, followed the craft in his own boat, which he shared with his wife Kham-Phiou and their daughter Thong-Samouth. They were accompanied by two boatmen and a cook.

At that time, the level of the Mekong River, inflated by the monsoon rains, was sufficient to ensure easy navigation, including the passage of the three rapids on the route. Against all odds, the crossing of Kaeng Luang[6], the 'Great Rapid', was dramatic. Despite the reputation for excellence of its crew, the craft carrying the royal objects, was badly positioned at the entrance to the channel, and was overturned.

The boatmen and royal guards, good swimmers, managed to climb on to the rocks, but the cargo, including bronze drums, gongs, gold and silver ritual cups, spears, sabres and elephant tusks set with silver, sank completely into the river. This accident was interpreted as a very bad omen for both the monarchy and the new state.

Phya Kham-Ouane died in 1948. He was already in poor health when he returned from Calcutta and Kunming and was possibly further affected by the tragic death of his son. Because of his rank and his meritorious services to his country, by royal decree his funeral were presided over by Prince Kham-Mao, the younger son of the

Nang Phya Kham-Phiou, daughter Thong-Samouth and a friend visiting That Luang stupa in Vientiane in 1947.

king and husband of Princess Kham-La, the younger sister of Prince Souvanna Phouma. The procession was accorded the distinction of being accompanied by the small Court Orchestra *(seb noy⁷)* and a detachment of Franco-Lao forces.

After his death, the name 'Muang Phaen' which had been reserved for the male line of his family was never to be bestowed again by the king on another aristocratic family.

The military and religious processions for the funeral of Kham-Ouane Muang Phaen, Phya Ratana Koumphon.

Nang Phya Kham-Phiou and her daughter Thong-Samouth.
Above, standing on the left side of the coffin is Tiao Kham-Mao.

Widowed at the age of thirty-five, Kham-Phiou decided the following year to commission a *Phra Bot* in gold leaves, representing the 28 Buddhas to decorate the wall at the back of the Great Buddha in Vat Sieng Mouane temple. According to traditional belief a thirty-six anniversary could be either a good or a bad omen. So in order to counter the ill fortune that had dogged her since the death of her husband, she decided to acquire merit by sponsoring religious donations or festivals. In order to avoid the agony she was suffering in her present situation, on ordinary days Kham-Phiou devoted her time to pious good works or religious retreats, following the Buddhist calendar and participated in numerous pilgrimages in Laos and to neighbouring countries with friends and relatives, organised by her cousins, Sathou Kham-Fan, the Abbot of Vat Khili, and Sathou Kham-Chan, the Abbot of Vat Saen. From time to time she visited France to see her daughter who was studying there.

Besides her religious activities, Kham-Phiou was often invited to the Royal Palace not merely for the game of *phai tong* but to assist in the making of pyramids of flowers on family or religious festivals, something in which she excelled. There, she met her relatives, in particular her second cousin Queen Kham-Phoui – their paternal

At a religious ceremony in Luang Prabang.

grandmothers had been sisters – with whom she had been very close since her childhood.

After the signing of the Franco-Lao General Agreement of 19 July 1949, recognising the independence of Laos, Souvanna Phouma, like all the leaders of the Lao Issara, returned to Laos, with the exception of Phetsarath who made his return conditional on the king restoring his title of Viceroy and Souphanouvong, who with the support of the Vietnamese leader Ho Chi Minh, created the Neo Lao Hak Sat (Lao Patriotic Front) to eradicate the French colonial authority in Indochina.

In 1954, when the armistice agreements in Geneva put an end to the Indochina War, the international situation took on a new dimension with the proclamation of the People's Republic of China on 1 October 1949 and the commitment of the United States in the war against the newly founded Democratic Republic of North Vietnam. Given its geographical location, in the heart of Indochina, Laos became the main stake for both sides.

In parallel, as much as Kham-Phiou's life was absorbed by family and religious matters, the personal situation of Souvanna Phouma in Laos at this moment in time was paradoxically but admirably adapted

In Yangon, at the celebration of the Maha Pasana Guha Cave where the 6th Buddhist Council was held in May 1956. With her relatives, from left to right: Nang Phya Kham-Phiou (Muang Chan), Nang Phya Kham-La, Nang Phya Kham-Sao.

With family and friends.

With her childhood friend Nang Bongmad Phimmasone.

to the actual situation. In the absence of his elder brother Phetsarath, he was regarded as the dominant figure of the Front Lineage, while from a political perspective, the esteem in which His Majesty Sisavang Vong held him, put him in a privileged position. Instinctively he recognised that his long-awaited moment had come; that moment of which he had dreamed since childhood in which he could make a major contribution to his country.

His political rise was dazzling: Minister of Public Works in 1951, he was promoted to Prime Minister the following year, and would remain so most of the time until 1975, with the mandate of an external policy of strict neutrality and that of internal national reunification. Unfortunately, given the regional situation, the mandate in question proved unworkable and the coalition government, formed following a new conference in Geneva in 1962 could not hold.

In the early 1970s, the American B52 bombings began in North Laos and North Vietnam. China responded with the creation of a common Indochinese front in Beijing. A special status was reserved for Laos that also stipulated respect for the throne.

The end of the Vietnam War signed on 27 January 1973 by the United States and North Vietnam in Paris, led to the ceasefire agreement in Laos that was reached on 12 February.

The Lao People's Democratic Republic (Lao PDR) was proclaimed in Vientiane on December 2, 1975.

Prince Souphanouvong was named as President with the ex-king becoming his counsellor, while Kaysone Phomvihane was appointed the General Secretary of the Lao People's Revolutionary Party (LPRP), as leader of the Government, with Souvanna Phouma as his counsellor.

Epilogue

A toast to the reunited couple and regaining lost time

"Let us raise our glasses to toast the former husband and the new bride, let us raise our glasses to toast the new husband and the former bride."[1]

With these subtle phrases Queen Mother Kham-Fan, surrounded by all Souvanna Phouma's family, notably his elder sister, Princess Sa-Ngiem Kham and three other princesses: one from the Great Lineage and two from the Front Lineage, as well as Luang Prabang Provincial Government officials, proposed a toast to the recent reunion of Prince Souvanna Phouma and Mom Kham-Phiou. This occurred in April 1979 in Luang Prabang in Souvanna Phouma's own house built in 1971 of stone and cement, in front of the elegant Downstream Mansion which itself had succumbed to time and termites.

These senior personages considered Kham-Phiou as one of themselves and despite the departure of Souvanna Phouma for Vientiane in July 1931, agreed with the Queen Mother's view that since Souvanna Phouma and Kham-Phiou had not been formally divorced, they were still married. Indeed, according to tradition, marriage with a secondary woman did not obliterate the legitimacy of the main wife.

The Queen Mother Kham-Fan and Prince Souvanna Phouma had a great regard for each other. The Queen Mother valued him for his academic success which had proved that a Laotian was just as capable as a Frenchman and also for his courageous struggle for their country's good. He valued her for her remarkable presence and for her nobility of character. He loved to recount how at the great reception in 1949[2]

Mom Kham-Phiou wearing a Royal Court attire, Luang Prabang 20th October 1960.

given in honour of His Majesty King Sisavang Vong by French President Auriol, the Queen had been the only woman in the Lao delegation not to be impressed by the splendours of the French Republic.

Apart from this the Queen Mother had a deep affection for Kham-Phiou, appreciating her simplicity, her tranquil manner and her cheerfulness. A third person was also dear to Kham-Phiou, Princess Saeng Sourichan, a half-sister of Souvanna Phouma who, as was mentioned earlier, was a teacher and the person who had taught Kham-Phiou to read and write in both Lao and French.

The affection in which the Queen Mother held Kham-Phiou had earned her the reproaches of her own family especially over the game of *phai tong* where Kham-Phiou was always her chosen partner.

"Your Majesty," it was said reproachfully, "you do not show the same preference for your closest nieces."

"Quite true," she had replied honestly. "I like having Kham-Phiou beside me. She always remains calm and whether she wins or loses she remains even tempered. When she loses she merely smiles."

Queen Kham-Fan also permitted Kham-Phiou a surprising freedom of speech as for example on the marriage of one of her step-sons to a princess of high rank when the couple were impossibly ill suited. The attitude and character of the prince clashed with the beauty and bearing of his future wife and Kham-Phiou, daring to express the general view, remarked to the Queen Mother that the royal princess was very beautiful and irreproachable in every way. The Queen Mother understood the underlying message but unwilling to acknowledge it, replied with a little laugh that this was true but that her step-son too was handsome.

Appreciating the sincere and naive nature of Kham-Phiou she did not impose strict protocol on her. When Kham-Phoui – at that time still styled 'princess' – heard of the conversation she was stunned as much by her cousin's audacity as by the tolerant reaction of her royal mother-in-law.

On numerous occasions Souvanna Phouma would come into contact with Kham-Phiou, either at official ceremonies or when the Government came to Luang Prabang, for Lao New Year in April when they paid their respects to the king or for the pirogue races on the ninth month (August- September) at the end of the rainy season, or at family gatherings in princely houses.

During one of these, Kham-Phiou refused after lunch, to take part in playing *phai tong* making the excuse that she had no money. Souvanna Phouma who had been watching her, jumped at the opportunity and slid a banknote into her hand, saying "play for me." There was an immediate cry of approval in the room. But Kham-Phiou, true to her resolution made on the occasion of their painful encounter in 1942, sought to avoid every such situation.

Despite the years of separation, the memory of the Prince remained vivid in Kham-Phiou's heart and thoughts. One day, on the occasion of Pimay in the middle of the 1960s, one of Souvanna Phouma's sons asked Thong-Samouth to introduce him to her mother, because his father had told him about his first wife. When Kham-Phiou saw him, she barely restrained her surprise and emotion, so great was his resemblance to her first husband. But she noticed that "the Prince was much more handsome, because he had beautiful skin", while his son was annoyingly pimply!

Later relations between Souvanna Phouma and his Eurasian wife deteriorated. He was totally dedicated and absorbed by his demanding political mission and had little time to spare for his family. His wife preferred living in France and only came back to Laos on short visits.

In 1967 they were formally divorced.

The following year Souvanna Phouma asked a woman in his entourage to invite Kham-Phiou to resume their married life. This proposal received a categorical refusal from Kham-Phiou's daughter. The attitude of the latter was not due to any dislike of Souvanna Phouma. On the contrary, their relations were excellent; Souvanna Phouma considered her as his own daughter and presented her as such to the public. Her opposition arose from her awareness of the previous appalling ill treatment her mother had suffered.

Thus it was only after the death of his Eurasian wife in 1977 and the departure from Laos of the children of both marriages, that the couple were finally able to come together again.

Learning of Kham-Phiou's presence in Vientiane, Souvanna Phouma addressed the following message to her: "Kham-Phiou, they have all gone, do not remain alone, come and live with me. Now there is no one to interfere."

Kham-Phiou accepted under two conditions: that a close relative of Souvanna Phouma should come for her, because she thought that as they had been separated for such a long time yet still married, it was not proper for a lady to go alone to a man's house. And that despite the government opposition to religious worship[3], she should be allowed to continue to offer morning rice to the monks and to pray and attend worship at the temple. Souvanna Phouma agreed to all the conditions and sent his younger sister Princess Kham-La to fetch her. In fact, Kham-Phiou

Letter of Prince Souvanna Phouma to his step-daughter telling about his daily life in Vientiane.

thought that he would send Princess Kinda[4] with whom she got along well. But she saw it as a mark of consideration from him that he sent his full sister from the same father and mother instead of his half-sister.

Therefore, when she moved to the Km3 residence on the Mekong river bank at the end of 1978, the installation of Mom Kham-Phiou was celebrated by a grand luncheon with close relatives and friends from the Public Health Department of Prince Souvanna Phouma, including Prince Souphanouvong, then President of the Lao People's Democratic Republic, his wife and their children.

The solemn meal breathed happiness. A couple of Souvanna Phouma's nephews who were very attached to Kham-Phiou, found it hard to contain their joy at this unexpected reunion. In their youth, they themselves had fled Luang Prabang in order to marry secretly without their parents' consent.

Kham-Phiou found an ever-loving and always courteous husband, now so tolerant and understanding that she hardly recognised him as the same person. Her joy was so great that she was speechless. After almost half a century apart what was there to say or do? The actual fact of being together after years of being alone seemed unreal.

Strange as it may seem, Kham-Phiou had not forgotten the least detail of their previous life together, as this story makes clear. Day after day she had recalled all the details, not only the suffering but the moments of joy when they escaped to the countryside away from the family fetters. Souvanna Phouma himself recalled the first moments of their meeting at the New Year festival in 1930 in Luang Prabang and how he had immediately fallen in love and his iron determination to marry her. He even found the camera he was carrying during that famous day. Although it no longer worked, the fact that he had found it was enough to move Kham-Piou.

For his part, Souvanna Phouma had found a wife as true to herself as before. Not only did she continue to give alms to the monks, but she also scrupulously followed the traditional calendar of auspicious and non-auspicious days in her daily life, as he had noticed in the first two years of their life together.

Over these long years one doubt had, however, continually gnawed at him: now was the time to resolve it.

"Kham-Phiou," he asked delicately, "why did you not come to join me in Vientiane?"

"I did my utmost to do so," she answered, her eyes filling with tears. "But when your sister-in-law sent an insulting letter threatening me if I should dare to come to Vientiane, my mother forbade me to go. I then wrote to you begging you to come yourself and fetch me. When I got no reply, for the first time in my life I disobeyed my mother and with the help of my friend Onesy I got ready to come to you secretly... But alas, fearing my flight, my mother had bribed the captain of the mail boat to refuse me passage. Only later did I learn that he had already been bribed by your sister-in-law to intercept and pass on to her my letters to you and the cigarettes I had made and sent for you. By contrast the letters you sent me at Hong Taeuy were delivered. So I could not understand why you ignored my plea to you to come and fetch me."

Souvanna Phouma now recalled having seen the driver smoking cigarettes identical to those which Kham-Phiou rolled, but at the time he had not enquired about their origin. Kham-Phiou's explanation made him understand that the situation had been far more complicated than he had realised and that it was not simply the case that in obedience to her mother she had failed to rejoin him. On the other hand, this separation had perhaps saved his wife from a fatal destiny, for the entourage of the princely mansion of his sister-in-law rustled with rumours of the brutal death – probably by poisoning – of a guilty maid for having borne two children to a prince of the Front Lineage.

"My frustrated departure," she continued, "was terrible. Helpless and believing I had now lost you forever, I wanted to die and begged Buddha to open the ground and bury me for all time."

Recalling his ultimatum that was meant to force her to come to Vientiane, Souvanna Phouma was overcome by sincere regret and felt enormous compassion for her.

Looking into each other eyes, and measuring the immensity of the lost years, the old couple both wept.

"We did not quarrel," stated Souvanna Phouma, "we did not divorce. Only we lived our lives apart. It was our families who did everything to separate us."

Kham-Phiou thought that as far as she was concerned, for nearly half a century she had been longing for a cherished dream that had escaped her. Her prayers had ultimately been heard and now the effects of the karma of her previous lives had ended for real. Does not Lao tradition state that the spouse who dies by your side in old age is the one to whom you are truly destined?

Appendix

Chronology of historical events
(1940-1975)

As the Second World War raged in Europe, Japan had been planning her expansion in the Asia-Pacific region. Through her alliance with Germany in 1940 she obtained permission from the French Government of Vichy to cede to Thailand the Lao provinces of Champassak and Sayaboury.

France compensated His Majesty Sisavang Vong, King of Luang Prabang for the loss of the latter by incorporating the provinces of Houa Khong, Xieng Khouang and Vientiane. Concurrently, by the same means used by Germany, Japan obtained permission from France to equip the Indochinese coasts with a long strategic system, from August 1940 to July 1941.

In Laos, at the initiative of France, Prince Phetsarath obtained from King Sisavang Vong the position of Viceroy, like his father, Prince Bounkhong, who died in 1920. A royal government was constituted, composed of a Prime Minister, in this case Prince Phetsarath, and four ministers. This transformation took place partially at the expense of the Crown Prince, Savang Vatthana, who lost his function as General Secretary of the Palace.

At a time when French authority was in decline, the titles and functions granted by the French to Prince Phetsarath (Viceroy, Prime Minister and President of the Buddhist Council) made him the most powerful man in all the Lao territories.

The Japanese invasion plan was put into effect following the lightning Pearl Harbour attack on 7th December 1941 which destroyed the American Navy in the Pacific and exposed a substantial area of Southeast Asia and part of the Asia-Pacific area to Japanese domination lasting until the end of 1943. The reaction of the Allies, in particular that of the United States after January 1944, forced the occupying Japanese forces to retreat northward. It was at this stage in the conflict that on 9th March 1945, in order to counter the Allied advance, Japan replaced the French colonial power in Indochina, and in order to stir up ill-feeling, urged the three countries of Laos, Vietnam and Cambodia to emancipate themselves.

Crown Prince Savang Vatthana in Luang Prabang issued a call to the people to resist the Japanese invasion but the Viceroy Phetsarath in Vientiane, backed by the invaders, formed a government in Vientiane and named himself as Prime Minister. The Japanese reached Luang Prabang on 5th April 1945 and, exiling the Crown Prince to Saigon, forced King Sisavang Vong to recognise the government of Phetsarath and to declare the independence of his kingdom from France, on 8th April 1945.

On 15th August 1945 following the American nuclear strikes on Hiroshima and Nagasaki, on 6th and 9th August, Japan capitulated. As a result of the Inter-Allied Potsdam Agreement in the same month, in both Vietnam and Laos to the north of the 16th parallel, the Chinese Nationalist Army disarmed Japanese troops who had occupied the whole of Indochina for nearly six months.

Given the new geo-political situation, the king, unlike Prince Phetsarath, who wanted to maintain the independence of the country and immediately achieve the unification of the Lao territories, felt that these objectives should be reached over time and with consensus. He accepted that his country should regain its former status as a French protectorate. In reaction to this position, Prince Phetsarath proclaimed the unification of all Lao territories. This initiative earned him the withdrawal of his title of Viceroy and his function as Prime Minister of the Government of Luang Prabang.

At that time there existed small opposition parties against the colonial authorities. These groups, composed of the Lao intelligentsia, who had been educated in French schools and universities, were rightly aware of their capacities and were united by their resentment of the French colonial administration's prejudices and the unequal treatment of qualified Laotian staff as compared to similarly qualified French nationals. Prince Souvanna Phouma, a full brother and Prince Souphanouvong[1], a half brother of Prince Phetsarath joined the movement.

In opposition to this movement, which could be described as progressive, was a conservative group loyal to the Throne and France, composed of princes and aristocrats employed in executive positions in the administration but usually lacking a university education. An example of this latter group was Prince Kindavong, like Prince Souphanouvong a half brother of Souvanna Phouma but by another mother. He had responded to the Crown Prince's appeal to resist the Japanese invasion by leaving his post as Governor of Phongsaly province and directing Franco-Lao resistance in Luang Prabang Kingdom.

On the 10th October 1945, after federating the progressive groups into a People's Assembly, Prince Phetsarath created the Lao Issara movement ('Free Laos') in Vientiane.

On the 13th October 1945, the People's Assembly drafted a Provisional Constitution which served as a legal tool to declare the deposition of the king and the formation of a Constituent Assembly and a government led by a native of Luang Prabang, Phanya Kham-Mao, the Governor of the province of Vientiane. These two institutions were created within the framework of a new State, the 'The State of Free Laos' (Pathet Lao Issara), of which Prince Phetsarath was to be the leader.

The deposition of the king, proclaimed by the Prime Minister on 20th October, was effected on the 4th November 1945 by a local commando against the Royal Palace in Luang Prabang. On this occasion, its leader, another native of Luang Prabang, stole the Royal Treasury under threat.

By the beginning of March 1946 the French-Lao resistance forces were re-occupying the country from the South. Distraught, the

Kham-Mao Government tried, against the advice of the Head of State, to obtain a peaceful compromise, but in vain. On the 23rd April 1946, in Luang Prabang, the government reinstalled the king as the 'constitutional monarch of unified Laos'. It was a waste of time: the arrival of the Franco-Lao forces the following day, with the exception of Prince Souphanouvong, who was organising the armed resistance in the center and the south of the country, provoked the exile of the Lao Issara leaders to Thailand with their families. They were welcomed by the two successive anti-colonialist governments of Pridi Banomyong and Thamrong Navasavat.

France, having re-established its rule in Laos, while continuing its policy of regrouping territories around the Luang Prabang monarchy established in 1893, was slowly guiding the country on the path to Independence.

The Constitutional Assembly, following elections held on the 11th November 1946 in the eleven Laotian provinces, ratified the formation of a temporary government whose presidency was conferred by the king on Prince Kindavong.

On the 11th May 1947 the reunited country was accorded a constitutional parliamentary monarchy whose first government was presided over by Prince Souvannarath, husband and half-brother of Princess Sa-Ngiem Kham and, as stated earlier, also the half-brother of Souvanna Phouma. In August of that same year it was decided the new State should be called 'Laos'.

On the 19th July 1949 the Franco-Lao General Convention recognised the independence of Laos and its association, on the same footing as France, within the French Union.

The council of Lao Issara considered these new developments were sufficient to justify their return: the only two exceptions being Prince Phetsarath who only came back in 1957 after the king had restored his title of Viceroy and Prince Souphanouvong who followed the pattern of the Viet Minh 'Front for Independence' of Ho Chi Minh and with their support created Neo Lao Hak Sat ('Lao Patriotic Front') to fight the French colonial authorities in Laos.

The proclamation on the 1st October 1949 of the People's Republic of China changed the face of regional politics. Henceforth China was in a position to support in practical ways the fight of the Viet Minh for total independence of the three countries of the French Union.

On the other hand, the United States which in 1950 had officially recognised the independence of the three countries, in 1954 took on a new role. In that same year when the Agreement for the Armistice in Indochina were signed in Geneva, it created SEATO², a politico-military organisation forming real strategic corridors extending from South Korea to Pakistan.

With this new configuration, the anti-colonial struggle in Indochina became engulfed in a battle between two Titans holding totally opposed doctrines and the domination of Laos became a vital strategic goal.

On his return to Laos, Prince Souvanna Phouma's political rise was meteoric: in 1951 he was Minister for Public Works, the next year he became Prime Minister with a mandate for strict neutrality internationally and for national reunification internally.

Despite enormous difficulties, with the agreement of his half-brother Prince Souphanouvong, he was able to set out a plan for the integration of Pathet Lao troops into the national army, and in 1957 and 1958 to organise elections with the aim of renewing at a national level the members of the National Assembly.

Unhappily these developments coincided with the period where the war efforts of the United States and their collaborators in Laos reached fever point. The Laotian right wing was disturbed by the electoral success of the left wing (the representatives of the Pathet Lao and their sympathisers) winning 20 seats out of 59.

Incited by the United States the Right now created the Committee for the Defence of National Interests (CDNI) led by General Phoumi Nosavan and was granted exceptional powers to prevent the rise of the Left. In July 1958 Souvanna Phouma was stripped of his post and functions and replaced by the rightist Phoui Sananikone.

On the 9th August 1960 a coup d'état organised by a neutralist,

Kong Le, a captain in the parachute regiment, returned Souvanna Phouma to power but by this action plunged the country into civil war. The Right continued to be upheld by the United States and with the active support of Thailand, retook by force the capital and formed a new government led by a southern Lao prince, Boun Oum.

Driven from Vientiane, Kong Le, now promoted to General, led his troops to the strategic position of the Plain of Jars in the northeast of Laos and established himself there. Laos was now divided into three politico-military movements, each led by a prince: the Centre pro-neutrality by Souvanna Phouma, the Left by Souphanouvong and the Right by Boun Oum.

The situation was becoming so dangerous to peace in the region that in 1962 the authorities overseeing the Geneva Agreement of 1954 called a fresh meeting of the States concerned. On the 23rd July of the same year the neutrality of Laos was not only re-affirmed but its precise rights and duties with regard to other countries were also explicitly laid down.

Before the 1962 conference, on the 4th June 1961, the leaders of the three Laotian movements, urged by Presidents Kennedy and Khrushchev, had met in Vienna and later in Zurich on the 22nd June of the same year. They agreed to form a coalition government with Prince Souvanna Phouma as President and Prince Souphanouvong and Prince Boun Oum as Vice-Presidents. This unusual initiative was warmly welcomed and applauded by the conference.

The positive results of this conference and the unexpected formation of the coalition government gave the Lao population real hope of peace and national union. And to further demonstrate this, in February 1963 King Savang Vatthana, who had inherited the Lao throne after his father's death in 1959, paid a courtesy visit to the countries who were signatories to the Geneva Accords.

Alas, just as in 1958, despite all the international efforts to produce peace and the determination of Souvanna Phouma to fulfil his political mandate, the battles on the ground could not be stopped. Backed by their respective sponsors the pro-American Right and the pro-Communist Left, worked intensively to extend their own zones of occupation. Caught in a vice, by 1966 the neutral troops, either defeated or absorbed into one or other camp were dissolved. Forced in 1967 to abandon his post to his opponent Phoui Sananikone, Souvanna Phouma was nevertheless returned to power the following year as leader of a new Right grouping which included the elected neutralist delegates. He retained that position up till the Communist victory in 1975.

The beginning of the 1970s saw the B52 American bombing of North Laos and North Vietnam and was equally the period during which the left wing groupings in the three Indochinese countries reunited by China in Beijing, formed a common front – 'to fight till a final victory is achieved'.

On the 6th March 1970, China and the Neo Lao Hak Sat (Lao Patriotic Front) agreed to give Laos a particular status based on five main points in accordance with the Geneva Accords of 1962, one of which was respect for the Throne (point 3), which Souvanna Phouma accepted in 1972.

In 1975 to escape the dominance of China and take control of its own future and decide alone the future of Indochina, North Vietnam turned to the Soviet Union. Thus the Laotian extreme Left put into practice what was subsequently known as 'the plan within the plan' *(phaen sone phaen[3])* by invading Vientiane on 28th April.

Following this takeover the Provisional Government of National Unity and the Consultative Political Council were both abolished. On the 1st and 2nd of December a National Congress in Vientiane declared the King had abdicated and then installed the Lao People's Democratic Republic (LPDR).

Footnotes

Foreword

1 ວ້ງຫຍ້ງ.

2 ວ້ງຫັ້ງ.

3 ວ້ງຫຍ້ງ.

4 ວ້ງການ.

5 ອຸຕຍາດ.

6 ກິມ.

7 ກິມພະວ້ງ.

8 ກິມມະອຸບ.

9 ກິມມະຫາດເລິກ.

10 ກິມມະສາງ.

11 ກິມມະບາ.

12 ກິມພະມ້າ.

13 ກິມມະຂ້າງ.

14 ກິມສິພາຍ.

15 ກິມພະຫັມ.

16 ເພັຽ.

17 ພຍາ.

18 ບາເຫມືອ.

19 ບາໄຕ້.

20 ເມືອງຂວາ.

21 ເມືອງຊ້າຍ.

22 ເມືອງການ.

23 ຫັ້ນຫັ້ງ.

24 ເຈົ້າພຍາ.

25 ເຈົ້າພຍາເມືອງຂວາ.

26 ເຈົ້າພຍາຫຍ້ງ.

27 ເຈົ້າພຍາຫຍ້ງເມືອງແສບ. Cf. *Khamphi phathammasad bouran (kod may kao khong lao)* [Manuscript of ancient traditions (Lao Customary Law)] ຄັມພິພະຫັມມະສາດບຸຍານ (ກິດໝາຍຂວງລາວ), p. 12.

28 ເຈົ້າພຍາຫຍ້ງເມືອງຈັນ. Cf. *ibid*, p. 13.

29 ເຈົ້າພຍາຫຍ້ງ ເມືອງແພບ. cf. *ibid*, p. 13.

30 ເຈົ້າ.

31 ເຈົ້າແຂວງ.

32 ນາຍແຂວງ.

33 ເຈົ້າເມືອງ.

34 ນາຍກອງ.

35 ຕາແສງ.

36 ນາຍບ້ານ.

37 ແກ້ວ, ຄູນ, ຈັນ, ແສງ, ສິງ, ສຸກ, ຂາວ, ສີ, ແດງ, ດຳ, ດີ, ດ້ວງ, ຕາ, ຕັນ, ຕີ, ຕຸ້ນ, ທິ, ບຸ່, ບໍ່ວ, ປານ, ປັນ, ເປ້ຍ, ປ້ອງ, ພັນ, ເພັ້ງ, ແພງ, ເພັຽ, ເຜີຍ, ຜາຍ, ຜູຍ, ຜິອ, ຜູ, ຝັ້ນ, ຟອງ, ມ້າວ, ຫັ້ນ, ມີ, ເຫັ້ກ, ຫ້າ, ອ້ອນ, ອິ້ນ, ອຸ່ນ, ແຫອ່ນ.

38 ຄຳ.

39 ທອງ.

40 ທ້າວ.

41 ນາງ.

42 ນາງເພັຽ.

43 ຫິວ.

44 ມ່ວນ.

45 ສາທຸ.

46 ສາທຸຍິ່ງ.

47 ເຈົ້າມ່ວນ.

48 ຈານ.

49 ອາຈານ.

50 ພະ.

51 ຫິຕ.

52 ຂວງ.

53 ຈິອ.

54 ບ່າວ.

55 ສາວ.

Prologue

1 Rama I (1782-1809), the founder of the Chakri Dynasty.

2 ເຈົ້າພຍາຫຍ້ງເມືອງແສບ.

3 ເຈົ້າພຍາຫຍ້ງ ເມືອງແສບແຫ້ຂວາ.

4 'ອອກທັບອອກເສິກ'. 'Out to fight, out to war'.

5 *hong* ໂຮງ 'mansion, residence, palace', *taeuy* ໃຕ້ 'south, downstream'.

6 'ກົນທ່ອງເມືອງ'. This meant that in terms of feudal rights and levy taxes he was entitled to half the city of Luang Prabang. After him, the title of Tiao Phanya Luang Muang Saen remained attached to the highest administrative functions but was only granted as a honorific title, carrying no entitlement to the prerogatives normally attached to the title.

7 These included tributes in kind: forest, fishery and agricultural products. Although nothing forced them to do so thereafter, the old vassals continued this practice towards the descendants of Tiao Phanya Luang Muang Saen Khaeo Khao until the mid-1940s.

8 ອັດຫົວຊຽງ.

9 ອັດຫາດ.

10 ເຕົ່າຫຍຸ.

11 ໜອງສະມຸດ. 'Sea lake'.

12 ໜອງຄຳ. 'Golden lake'.

13 ຂຽງແກ້ວ.

14 ບ້ານຄ້າຍ.

15 ບ້ານຄອຍ.

16 The creation of the function of Viceroy appeared during the kingdom of Ayutthaya in the first half of the fifteenth century.

17 Phanya Luang Muang Saen is mentioned in some historical works (cf. Auguste Pavie, 1898, p. 136; M.L. Manich Jumsai, 1971, p. 142).

Chapter 1

1 With the exception of certain Buddha statues, such as the Phra Bang, the palladium of the kingdom, which is only descended on the first day of the new year.

2 ບ້າງສິງພະ.

3 ປູ່ເຍີ່ຍເຍີ.

4 ສິງແກ້ວສິງໄກ.

5 ດອກຄຳ. *Thevetia neriifolia*.

6 ດອກຄຳຫມັ້າ. *Saraca thoreli*. 'Golden flower of Burma'.

7 ດອກນົ້. *Ochrocarpus siamensis*.

8 ດອກນົມງົວ. *Olax obtusa*. 'Cow breast flower'.

9 ດອກຂ້ອນ. *Jasminum sambac*.

10 ດອກໄຂ່ເນົ່າ. *Gardenia philastrei*. 'Rotten egg flower'. Also called *dok mok* (ດອກໝອກ), 'mist flower'.

11 ດອກອິຫຸບ. *Talauma mutabilis*.

12 ດອກຫວາຍເທິນ. *Hedychium coronarium*.

13 ດອກຕົ້ງ. *Hoya macrophylla*.

14 ຫວ້ານໄພ. *Zingiber zerumbet*.

15 ສົ້ມປ່ອຍ. *Acacia concinna*.

16 ສິນນາໆ.

17 ໂອ.

18 ຂັນ.

19 ອັນ.

20 The cornets of flowers symbolise the persons concerned; the candles, the sacral character of the act.

21 ຂ້ານ້າກັຖງ.

22 Prince Souvanna Phouma (1901-1984) was born in Luang Prabang. He was the fourth son of Viceroy Bounkhong and his second wife Princess Thong-Sy.

23 Prince Souvannarath was both a half-brother to Prince Souvanna Phouma and his brother-in-law, having married his half-sister Princess Sa-Ngiem Kham.

24 Kham-Phoui (1880-1925), Tiao Phanya Luang Mun Na ເຈົ້າພຍາທຫຼວງໝື່ນໜ້າ ('Great Lord of 10,000 faces') served as the First President of the Court of Appeal in Vientiane. He died at the age of 45. Early in his career in the 1900s he, as Phya Mun Na, administered Pak Tha district, at the mouth

of the Nam Tha River on the Mekong River, in Luang Namtha Province (cf. Alfred Raquez, 1902, p. 312).

25 ແມ່ນີມ.

26 Onesy later married Phya Sing, the Royal Master of Ceremonies.

27 ບ້ານນອກ.

28 ໝາກຂີ້ຫູດ. *Citrus hystrix*.

29 ຍັກຄີນີ.

30 ພູ່ທ້າວພູບາໆ.

Chapter 2

1 ແມ່ຊີ.

2 ລູກສາວຍັງນ້ອຍຍັງບໍ່ຮູ້ ຖ້ອຍຮູ້ຄວາມ ຍັງບໍ່ຮູ້ເຮັດຍູ່ເຮັດກິນ ຂອງໄພບ່າງພິ້ນ !'

3 'ແລ້ວແຕ່ທ່ອແມ່'.

4 ຂ້ານ້ອຍ.

5 ທຸ. Diminutive of *'sathou'* ສາທຸ.

6 ທ່ອ.

7 ຂ້ອຍ.

8 ເຈົ້າ.

9 ໂອຍ.

10 ໂຕ.

11 ລະບາດ.

12 ກອງ.

13 ຂີ້ອີ.

14 ຂີ້ອີ້.

15 ຂີງ.

16 ຂີມ.

17 ແຄບ.

18 ຂັບຂຸ້ມ.

19 ສະໝ້ອງສາມສ້າວ.

20 ອ່ານໝັ້ງສີ.

21 ເຫຼົ້າລາວ. Rice alcohol, also called 'water of courage and invulnerability' (*nam ka nam khong* ນ້ຳກ້ານ້ຳຄົງ), is present in mediumistic rites to connect the earth to the sky.

22 Nang Phya Kham-Douang, who was reluctant to exchange her metallic coins (gold, silver or bronze) for paper money, was severely penalised by the Public Treasury of Luang Prabang.

23 Equivalent to the monthly salary of a young secretary of Residence.

24 Siam took the name of 'Thailand' in 1939.

25 'ເອຶາກ່າງເອຶາ'.

Chapter 3

1 Approximately from June to August.

2 *'hae bao kheuy pai sou heuan sao phaeuy'* ແຫ່ບ່າວເຂີຍ ໄປສູ່ເຮືອນສາວໄພ້.

3 *'hae sao phaeuy pai sou hong'* ແຫ່ສາວໄພ້ໄປສູ່ໂຮງ.

4 *'sou khouan song thang'* ສູ່ຂ້ອນສອງທາງ.

5 And in particular cases from the aristocracy. In this case, after the 'procession in both directions' the bridegroom returns after a few days in his

house, to the bride's home and settles there.

6 *'sou khouan noy'* ສູ່ຂ້ອນນ້ອຍ.

7 *'sou khouan khan mak'* ສູ່ຂ້ອນຂັນໝາກ.

8 According to Lao belief, each individual possesses 32 souls distributed at different points of the body.

9 *'pha khouan sao phaeuy'* ພາຂ້ອນສາວໄພ້.

10 ພາຂ້ອນ.

11 The cup and bowl in question are used on numerous religious occasions, especially for the morning offerings to the monks. The one with a stem belongs to the man, and the one without to the woman. Their proximity in the present case symbolises the union of the future spouses.

12 ພາ. According to the rank and wealth of the family, the tray could be of bamboo, rattan, lacquered or in metal (bronze, silver).

13 This thread is used to tie together the wrists of the bride and groom.

14 ດອກຫອບໄກ່. *Celosia argentea*.

15 ດອກດາວເຮືອງ. *Tagetes*. 'Shining star flower'.

16 ໃບຄ້າໃບຄູນ. *Codiaeum variegatum*. 'To support leave-auspicious leave'.

17 ໃບເຈືງໃບຄຳ. *Codiaeum variegatum*. 'Silver- leaf-golden-leaf'.

18 ໃບດອກຮັກ. *Calotropis gigantea*. 'Love flower leaves'.

19 *Piper betle*.

20 ອັບພູ.

21 ດອກຮັກ. 'Love flower'.

22 ໝາກຈັບ. *Trapa bicornis*. 'Catch fruit'.

23 ບໍ່ແຮດ.

24 ງາຂົ້ງ.

25 ມິດດ້າມງາດ້າມເງິນ.

26 ມິດປາດໝາກ.

27 ມິດສະບາກ.

28 ກ້ອຍໄຂ່ບົ່ງຫວີ.

29 ເຂົ້າໜົມຂອງຕ້ອນ.

30 ເຂົ້າຕົ້ມ.

31 ເຂົ້າໂດຍ.

32 ເຂົ້າຂົ້ພູ.

33 ເຂົ້າໜົມຂົ້ນ.

34 ແອບເຂົ້າໝວຍ. Sticky rice is the basis of Lao food.

35 ຂັນໝາກ. The betel kit is the most convivial object par excellence. It is presented to visitors first, even before engaging in conversation. A complete betel kit (*kheuang khan mak khob soud* ເຄື່ອງຂັນໝາກຄົບຊຸດ) consists of a box of betel nut (*oup mak* ອູບໝາກ), a box of tobacco (*oup ya* ອູບຢາ), a box of lime (*bok poun* ບອກປູນ), a box

of betel leaves (*song phou* ຊອງພູ), a betel nut cracker (*mid sanak* ມິດສະນາກ), a knife with ivory or silver handle to peel the bark of the betel nut (*mid pad mak* ມິດປາດໝາກ) and a hollow rhinoceros horn filled with lip balm, essential to soften the harshness left on the lips by the mastication of the betel chew (*aeb nouad si pak* ແອບບວດສິປາກ).

36 ບ້າເຕົ້າເງິນ.

37 ເສື້ອກ້າຍ.

38 ສິ້ນ. In Luang Prabang the traditional Lao wrap-around skirt is composed of three separate parts: one upper part at waist level, called the 'top of the skirt' (*houa sin* ຫົວສິ້ນ), a middle part and a lower part, called 'bottom of the skirt' (*tin sin* ຕິນສິ້ນ). Each of these is made separately, in its appropriate style of decoration. It is for the purchaser to decide which part to match with which.

39 ຜ້າບ່ຽງ.

40 ສາຍຄ້ອງ.

41 ໝາກຕຸ້ມ.

42 ປັກໜິບ.

43 ດອກໂທອ.

44 ຕ້າງ.

45 ສາຍຄໍ.

46 ປອກແຂນກ້ຽງ.

47 ປອກແຂນຝັ້ນ.

48 ປອກແຂນກະຕ່ອຍ.

49 During the life of a Lao man, it is common to take the yellow robe and disrobe several times.

50 ໝໍພອນ.

51 In order to ensure prosperity, jewels must stay with the new couple a whole night.

Chapter 4

1 ເຈົ້າທິອ. 'Prince Honourable'. For some unknown reason, this name was specific to him. Was it due to his administrative functions or his bonds of kinship with the Royal family?

2 ເອາະຫງາມ.

3 ເຂົ້າປຸ້ນ.

4 ບ້າພິກ.

5 ເຫັດເຜາະ. *Astraeus hygrometricus*.

6 ບ້າງາ.

7 ບ້າແຈ່ວ.

8 ພັນໄຂ່.

9 ໝົກປາຟອກ.

10 ອໍ່ໝໄມ້.

11 ຂຸບຜັກ.

12 ຂຸບໝາກມ້ີ.

13 ປິ່ນໝາກເຂືອ.

14 ຂົ້ຮອປາແດກ.

15 ດອກແຄ. *Sesbania grandiflora*.

16 ໝົກດອກແຄ.

17 ລິ້ນໄມ້. *Oroxylum indicum*.

18 ໝີກໝາກລົ່ນໄມ້.

19 ໝີກດອກຂີ່ງ.

20 ສົ້ມໄລ່ປາ.

21 ກຸ້ງຍ່າງ.

22 ແຈ່ວຂີ່ງ.

23 ໝາກກອກ. *Spondias mangifera*.

24 ແຈ່ວໝາກກອກ.

25 ແຈ່ວຍອດຫວາຍ.

26 ແຈ່ວບວງ.

27 ໄພ້ຕອງ. One type of the Chinese money-suited playing cards, composed of 120 cards, very popular in Luang Prabang aristocratic circles.

28 In Vietnam.

29 Prince Bounkhong, deceased in 1920.

30 Prince Phetsarath, born in 1890, was a full brother to Prince Souvanna Phouma.

31 ບ້ານເຈັກ.

32 *sieng* ສຽງ 'sound'; *mouane* ມ່ວນ 'melodious'. The temple was built in 1853 by Phanya Sisonsay.

33 ແຂວນບາງ.

34 ພະບິດ.

Chapter 5

1 Auguste Pavie was the architect of the French protectorate over Laos, obtained after the Franco-Siamese treaty of 1893.

2 Cf. Grant Evans, *A Short History of Laos,* 2002, p. 49.

3 'ເອົາກັບເຈົ້າຕໍ່ງເອົາຄວາມ ເອົາເຂົ້າ ຢ່າເອົານາໃສ່ໃຈ'.

4 Company for the Study and Exploitation of Minerals of Indochina.

5 'ບາເບິ່ງໝີ້ແໝ... ມີແມງກອກກໄດ້ໄຟ'.

Chapter 6

1 *Pha tad kae* ຜາຕັດແກ້.

2 ເທອະດາ.

3 *Hid sib song khong sib si* ຮີດສິບສອງຄອງສິບສີ່.

4 Vat Pa Phai (ວັດປ່າໄພ່) = 'temple of the bamboo forest'. The temple was rebuilt in 1815 by Phya Samlat.

5 Also known as Vat Nyouang Ngeun Nyouang Kham (ວັດຍວງເງິນຍວງຄຳ).

6 ບຸນພະເວດ. 'Vet' is the contraction of *Vessantara*, the name of the Buddha during his penultimate reincarnation. Prince Vessantara is for Buddhists the ultimate model of charity and generosity. Also known as *boun mahasad* ບຸນມຫາຊາດ, 'feast of the great life'.

7 ບຸນກັບຖິມ.

8 ບອດພະຄູ່ອາຍຸ.

9 ບອດກອງຫົດ.

10 ຫ້ອຍຂົ້ນຫວດ.

11 7.5 g.

12 3.525 g.

13 'than pha khao kang heuan' ທາບພາເຂົ້າກາງເຮືອນ.

14 ບາດ.

15 In 1853.

16 ຫ້ມ.

17 ໝ້ວງສີຜູກ.

18 ກາລະເກດ.

19 ຂູ່ວັດ.

20 ອິນເໜິງ.

21 ພຸທະເສບ.

22 1885-1886.

23 ໝັບ. 1 *man* = 27 g.

24 ປູປາ.

25 ທຳຖ້ອ.

26 Kham-Sao was the eldest child of Onesy, Phanya Muang Saen, the President of the Tribunal in Luang Prabang (cf. Alfred Raquez, *Pages Laotiennes*, 1902, p. 174).

27 King Sakarin reigned from 1889 to 1904.

28 The seniority of aristocratic families of Luang Prabang could be dated based on the number of generations who had been holding 'kham' in their given names. At the birth of Kham-Pheng, his father, Chanpheng was titled Phya Muang Kang and worked at the Tribunal of Luang Prabang, so his son could have the prefix 'kham' added to his given name.

29 ປອກແຂນສິໝາງລູກ.

30 ປອກແຊບແຊກກັຽງ ແຊກກູດ.

Chapter 7

1 ເຮືອນຄູ່.

2 'ກິຊຍາກປູມເໜງລອຍບໍ່ໆ'.

3 ເງືອກ.

Chapter 8

1 ໃບພູ. *Piper betle*.

2 ເປືອກຫາດ. *Artocarpus asperula*.

3 ສີສຽດ. *Pentace burmanica*.

4 ໝາກ. *Areca catechu*.

5 ກ້ານພູ. *Eugenia aromatica*.

6 ວັຽງ.

7 ປັກກິ້ງ.

8 ຂັນຕາລະບັດ.

9 ໝອບເທ້າ.

10 'ຜູ້ໃດຖິ້ມເພັດຂອງບໍ່ເປັນ ແມ່ນບໍ່ມີສມອງ'.

11 ໂອຍ! ພໍ່ຄ້າໝາກທິບເອີຍ! ບໍ່ໄປຣອດໃສ່ຈັກເທື່ອແລ້ວ!'

12 'ເຈົ້າຮູ້ບ່ວ່າ ມີໃດ ພໍ່ຄ້າໝາກທິບພຸ້ນ ແຕ່ບ່ອນນີ້ໆ ເຮົາຈະ ນອນກັບນີ້ໆຢູ່ໆ ລູກຂ້ອຍ'ຫຼານ!'

Chapter 9

1 His Majesty Sisavang Vong (1920-1959).

2 ບ້ອຍ.

3 Kham-Phan, Tiao Kommasang, was in charge of the Royal Elephants Department and the father of Her Majesty Queen Kham-Phoui. His mother was the sister of Tiao Kham-Phiou, Kham-Phoui's (Tiao Phanya Luang Mun Na) mother.

4 'ໂອຍ! ເອີ້ນຜີວຂື້ງກໍ ໄດ້ແລ້ວ!'

Chapter 10

1 Now according to Lao beliefs to step over a person is not only a deadly insult but can also cause the departure of that person's inner souls and thus risk their death.

Chapter 12

1 Because of the dangers of attacks from Chinese pirates, the region of Phongsaly like some others regions in Tonkin bordering Yunnan had since 1916 been attached to Luang Prabang as a region administered by the French army (Ve territoire militaire).

2 According to one half-sister of His Majesty King Savang Vathana, Princess Kham-Pin, also a descendant of Tiao Phanya Luang Muang Saen Khaeo Khao through her mother Mom Kham-Thip, this naming was due to the fact that her ancestor did not chew betel nut and therefore had not the characteristic red colour.

3 'Vat pak khan' = 'temple of the mouth of the Nam Khan River'. The temple was built in 1737 by Phanya Chanthep.

4 In popular circles, the youngest children are generally the most favoured.

5 ຫາມ.

6 Chao Kham Lu (1884-1924), cf. Foon Ming Liew-

7 Herres, 'Intra-dynastic and Inter-Tai Conflicts in the Old Kingdom of Moeng Lü in Southern Yunnan', *SOAS Bulletin of Burma Research* 5, 2007, p. 109.

8 ໝໍ່ເຢົາ.

9 'ແມ່ເທົ້າຫຍັງ? ໃຫ້ຮັ່ງຢແມ່?'

Chapter 13

1 Cf. Grant Evans, 2009, p. 160.

2 ເຮືອໂມະ. A set of two dugouts held parallel to each other like catamarans by a large raft whose length varies according to needs. On the latter were mounted a covered dwelling, a kitchen, and a bathroom.

3 ພະລັກພະລານ.

4 ບາງແກ້ວ.

5 ອີປ້ອກ.

6 ແກ້ງຫງອງ.

7 ເສບບ້ອຍ.

Epilogue

1 ʻຄົນເພື່ອຜີວເກົາ ເນື້ອໃໝ່, ຄົນເພື່ອຜີວໃໝ່ ເນື້ອເກົາʼ. In fact this story was well known to families in Luang Prabang (cf. Grant Evans, *A Short History of Laos*, 2002, p. 68; *The Last Century of Lao Royalty*, 2009, p. 155, although the author made a mistake about Kham-Phiou's identity).

2 The reception followed the signing of the Agreement confirming the independence of the Kingdom of Laos within the framework of the French Union on 19 July 1949.

3 It was only in 1987 that freedom of worship was officially restored.

4 Princess Chinda was of same father and mother with Prince Souphanouvong. She was therefore a half-sister of Prince Souvanna Phouma.

Appendix

1 Souphanouvong was born in 1909, the son of Bounkhong (Viceroy from 1890-1920) and Mom Kham-Ouane. Contrary to the assertions of some, the latter was not a servant of the Downstream Mansion, but the daughter of Tiao Muang of Pak Lay, a district not far from Luang Prabang. Her parents tried in vain to postpone Bounkhong's request for marriage, on the pretext that she was too young and their only daughter (*loukthok* ລູກທອກ). It was indeed rare for families at that time to have few children. At the third attempt, the Viceroy was finally able to marry her and made her his 11th and favourite concubine.

2 Southeast Asia Treaty Organisation.

3 ແຜນຂ້ອນແຜນ.

Glossary

aeb khao niaeo: traditional basket of sticky rice

aeb nouad si pak: hollow rhinoceros horn filled with lip balm, essential to soften the harshness left on the lips by the mastication of the betel chew

baeuy kham baeuy khoun: Codiaeum variegatum

baeuy ngeun baeuy kham: Codiaeum variegatum

baeuy phou: betel leaf

bao: man of common origin. The *bao* was in this capacity *corvéable* by the royal administration, but exempt from any chore if he were assigned to the service of a high official

baht: ancient monetary unit

bok poun: box of lime

bouad kong hod: consecration of a meritorious monk

bouad phra khou anyou: in order to celebrate one's own anniversary and to prolong one's own life one sponsors a number of individuals, the number equal to one's age plus one, to undertake a period as monks on the eighth month of the lunar calendar before the monsoon

boun kanthin: Buddhist festival on the eleventh month of the lunar calendar, to make donations of new clothes to monks after the rainy season.

boun phra vet or *boun mahasad:* Buddhist festival on the first month of the lunar calendar to celebrate the last life of Prince Vessantara before his illumination as a Buddha

chan (diminutive of *achan*): man who has returned to secular life after a period of ordination in adulthood during which he spent at least several Buddhist lengths as monk

dok dao heuang: Tagetes

dok hak: Calotropis gigantea

dok i houb: Talauma mutabilis

dok hone kai: Celosia argentea

dok khae: Sesbania grandiflora

dok khai nao: Gardenia philastrei

dok kham: Thevetia neriifolia

dok kham phama: Saraca thoreli

dok mok: Gardenia philastrei

dok no: Ochrocarpus siamensis

dok nom ngoua: Olax obtusa

dok say heun: Hedychium coronarium

dok sone: Jasminum sambac

dok tang: Hoya macrophylla

dok vai: traditional hairpin

ham: sedan chair

hed pho: Astraeus hygrometricus

heua mo: set of two dugouts held parallel to each other like catamarans by a large raft whose length varies according to needs. On the latter were mounted a covered dwelling, a kitchen, and a bathroom

hong taeuy: downstream mansion

houa: in Luang Prabang tradition, this term is more of the speaking register. Literally it means the 'head' which is the most sacred part of the body. Therefore this term is used to emphasise the aristocratic origin of the person in question and means 'the honourable'

i pok: Royal puppet troop

jiaeo bong: chili pepper and buffalo rind

jiaeo khing: ginger sauce

jiaeo mak kok: sauce with *mak kok* fruit

jiae nyod vay: sauce with rattan shoots

joua: novice

kan phou: clove. *Eugenia aromatica*

khaen: bamboo mouth organ

khaen nang: wooden console

kham: gold

khan: silver stem cup exclusively used for traditional ceremonies to carry the offerings

khan mak: betel kit

khan talabat: ceremonial fan

khanoy: 'your subject' to designate oneself when addressing to someone of higher status

khao khob: crispy rice cakes

khao khi nou: sweet made of fried rice flour caramelised with treacle

khao nom khong tone: traditional sweetmeats

khao nom san: cake made of steamed rice flour with several colours and layers

khao poun: traditional Luang Prabang rice vermicelli soup

khao tom: cake made of banana, sticky rice and coconut wrapped into banana leaves and steamed

kheuang khan mak khob soud: complete betel kit

khiaeo pa daek: pork rind fried with fish in brine

khim: cithar

kom: department

komma khoun: department in charge of the royal treasury

kom mahadlek: department in charge of the guard of the royal Palace

komma na: department in charge of the Royal rice fields

kom phama: department in charge of the royal horses

kom phamo: department in charge of the royal health.

kom pravang: department in charge of the affairs of the royal palace

komma sang: department in charge of the royal stores, provisions and weapons

komma sang: department in charge of the royal elephants

kom siphay: department in charge of the royal barges

kong: drum

kouay khai neung vi: a hand of 'egg' bananas

koung yang: smoked shrimp

lanat: xylophone

lao lao: rice alcohol

lin mai: Oroxylum indicum

mae nom: nanny

mae su: intermediary

mak: areca nut. *Areca catechu*

mak jab: Trapa bicornis

mak khi houd: Citrus hystrix

mak kok: Spondias mangifera

mak toum: traditional beads chain

man: ancient monetary unit

mid dam nga dam ngeun: pair of knives with ivory, silver or gold handle

mid pad mak: knife with ivory or silver

handle to peel the bark of the betel nut

mid sanak: betel nut cracker

mo phone: master of ceremonies

mo yao: shaman

mok dok khae: steamed papillotes of *dok khae* flower

mok dok khing: steamed papillotes of ginger buds

mok mak lin mai: steamed papillotes of *lin mai* fruits

mok pa fok: fish mousse

mom: aristocratic or common-law woman married to a nobleman

mone thao: triangular or rectangular shaped pillows

nam jiaeo: chili sauce

nam mouak: water that was used to soak sticky rice

nam pa: fish sauce

nam phik: coconut milk and chili broth

nam song phra: scented water to shower Buddha statues

nam tao ngeun: silver ewer

nang: term specific to women of the nobility and of the aristocracy

nang kaeo: Royal dancers

nang phya: wife of an aristocrat, whether her husband is titled *phya* or *phanya*

nay bane: chief of village

nay kong: chief of sub-district

nga sang: elephant tusk

ngeuak: serpentlike water spirit

ngiaeng: spittoon

no haed: rhinoceros horns

noy: small, 'little one'

nyakkhini: ogress

o: silver cup exclusively used for traditional ceremonies to carry the offerings

o: in Luang Prabang tradition, term used to refer to oneself when speaking to the servants

ok lam: traditional Luang Prabang dish combining different kinds of vegetables, shoots and wild plants, spices and meat cooked to different degrees

oua no mai: stuffed bamboo shoots

oub mak: box of betel nut

oub ya: box of tobacco

ouparat: viceroy

pak ding: Luang Prabang royal embroidery technique using gold or silver threads, purls and spangles

pak phom: traditional hairpin

peuak had: Artocarpus asperula

pha: traditional round tray

pha biaeng: traditional scarf

pha khouan: tray of the souls

phai tong: one type of the Chinese money-suited playing cards, composed of 120 cards, very popular in Luang Prabang aristocratic circles.

phan khai: small egg rolls stuffed with meat and steamed

phanya: the second title granted by the King to the higher officers of the army and administration

phou: Piper betle

phra: Buddhist monk

phra bot: mural or banner votive offerings representing the Buddha

phra lak phra lam: Lao *Ramayana*

phya: the first title granted by the King to the higher officers of the army and administration

pok khaen fan: traditional twisted bracelet

pok khaen katoy: traditional twisted bracelet

pok khaen kiaeng: traditional plain bracelet

pok khaen saek kiaeng saek koud: traditional bracelet

pok khaen si mak louk: traditional bracelet

pon mak kheua: eggplant melting in meat

sa nam kiaeng: traditional lacquered basket

salung: ancient monetary unit

sao: girl of common origin

sathou: abbot of a temple or prince of high rank

sathou nying: princess of high rank

say kho: traditional necklace

say khong: traditional hair chain

seb noy: small Court orchestra

seua pay: traditional double-breasted jacket

si siaed: Pentace burmanica

sin: traditional skirt

sing: cymbals

so i: viola

so ou: viola

som khai pa: fish eggs in brine

som poy: Acacia concinna

soma: ritual of homage to parents and older relatives

song phou: box of betel leaves

soub mak mi: steamed young jackfruit salad

soub phak: steamed vegetable shoots salad garnished with sesame seeds and ginger

tang: traditional earrings

tassaeng: chief of township

thao: term specific to noble and aristocratic men

thevada: deity

thid: man who has returned to secular life after a short period of ordination in adulthood

thong: gold

thou (diminutive of *sathou*): term used to

name monks or nobles

tiao: term indicating nobility

tiao houa: 'prince honourable'

tiao khouaeng (or *nay khouaeng):* governor of province

tiao mom: the first grade of a monk before becoming *sathou*

tiao muang: originally used to designate the lord of a principality but later applied to a mayor or chief of district

tiao phanya: the third title granted by the King to the higher officers of the army and administration

tiao phanya luang: the fourth and highest title granted by the King to the higher officers of the army and administration

to: in Luang Prabang tradition, term used by masters to address their servants

van: banana leaf cone filled with flowers and a pair of wax candles

van phai: Zingiber zerumbet

van phou: banana leaf cone filled with betel leaves

vang kang: Middle Lineage or Middle Palace

vang lang: Rear Lineage or Rear Palace

vang luang: Great Lineage or Great Palace

vang na: Front Lineage or Front Palace

xieng: child who has returned to secular life after a period of ordination in childhood

Bibliography

Thao Boun Souk, *Louang Phrabang: 600 ans d'art bouddhique lao, Bulletin des Amis du Royaume Lao,* Vientiane, 1974, 160 p.

Jean Deuve, *Guérilla au Laos,* Paris, L'Harmattan, 1997, 340 p.

Amphay Doré, *Le partage du Mékong,* Paris, Encre, 1980, 263 p.

Amphay Doré, *Aux sources de la civilisation lao : contribution ethno-historique à la connaissance et à la culture louang-phrabanaise,* thèse de doctorat d'Etat, 2 volumes, Sorbonne, Paris, Cercle de Culture et de Recherches Laotiennes, 984 p.

Grant Evans, *A Short History of Laos. The Land in Between,* Bangkok, Silkworm Books, 2002, 251 p.

Grant Evans, *The Last Century of Lao Royalty: A Documentary History,* Bangkok, Silkworm Books, 2009, 430 p.

Foon Ming Liew-Herres, 'Intra-dynastic and Inter-Tai Conflicts in the Old Kingdom of Moeng Lü in Southern Yunnan', *SOAS Bulletin of Burma Research* 5, 2007, p. 51-112.

Geoffrey C. Gunn, 'Lao Issara (Issarak)', p. 767-768, in *Southeast Asia: A Historical Encyclopedia from Angkor Wat to East Timor,* 3 volumes, Ooi Keat Gin (ed.), ABC-CLIO, 2004, 1791 p.

Mom Luang Manich Jumsai, *History of Laos,* Bangkok, Chalermit 1-2 Erawan Arcade, 1971, 325 p.

Khamphi phathammasad bouran (kod may kao khong lao) [Manuscript of ancient traditions (Lao Customary Law)] ຄັມພີພຣະຂັມມະສາດບູຮານ (ກົດໝາຍຂອງລາວ), Department of Literature, Literary Committee, Vientiane, 1956, 253 p.

Mom Kham-Phiou, letters written between 1979 and 1984 (family archives).

Pierre S. Nginn, 'Le Nouvel An Lao (Fêtes du 5e mois)', in *Présence du Royaume Lao, France-Asie,* Tome XII, 1956, p.946-948.

Auguste Pavie, *Recherche sur l'histoire du Cambodge, du Laos et du Siam,* Mission Pavie II, Paris, Ernest Leroux, 1898, 449 p. Alfred Raquez, *Pages Laotiennes,* Hanoi, Schneider, 1902, 537 p.

Général G. Sabattier, *Le destin de l'Indochine, souvenirs et documents 1941-1951,* Paris, Plon, 1952, p. 197.

Katay D. Sasorith, 'Comment joue-t-on le Phay-Tong ?', in *Présence du Royaume Lao, France-Asie,* Tome XII, 1956, p. 879-886.

Phia Sing, *Traditional Recipes of Laos,* London, Prospect Books, 1981, 318 p.

Tiao Souvanna Phouma, letters written betwen 1979 and 1983 (family archives).

Lieutenant-colonel Tournier, *Notice sur le Laos français,* Imprimerie F.-H. Schneider, Hanoi, 1900, 191 p.

Jules Vidal, *Noms vernaculaires de plantes (lao, mèo, kha) en usage au Laos, Bulletin de l'École Française d'Extrême-Orient,* Tome 49, n°2, 1959, p. 435-608.

Andrew Walker, *The Legend of the Golden Boat: Regulation, Trade, and Traders in the Border- lands of Laos, China, Thailand and Burma.* Richmond, Curzon Press, 1999, 232 p.

Marcel Zago, *Rites et cérémonies en milieu bouddhiste lao, Documenta Missonalia* 6, Roma, Università Gregoriana Editrice, 1972, 408 p.

Family Trees

PATERNAL GENEALOGY OF
KHAM-PHIOU

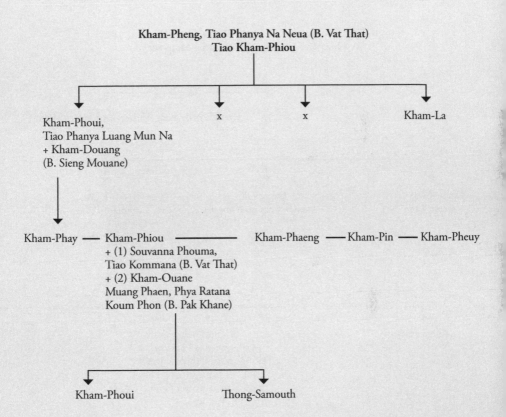

Kham-Pheng, Tiao Phanya Na Neua (B. Vat That)
Tiao Kham-Phiou

Kham-Phoui,
Tiao Phanya Luang Mun Na
+ Kham-Douang
(B. Sieng Mouane)

x   x   Kham-La

Kham-Phay —— Kham-Phiou ———————— Kham-Phaeng —— Kham-Pin —— Kham-Pheuy
+ (1) Souvanna Phouma,
Tiao Kommana (B. Vat That)
+ (2) Kham-Ouane
Muang Phaen, Phya Ratana
Koum Phon (B. Pak Khane)

Kham-Phoui   Thong-Samouth

Family Trees

MATERNAL GENEALOGY OF
KHAM-PHIOU

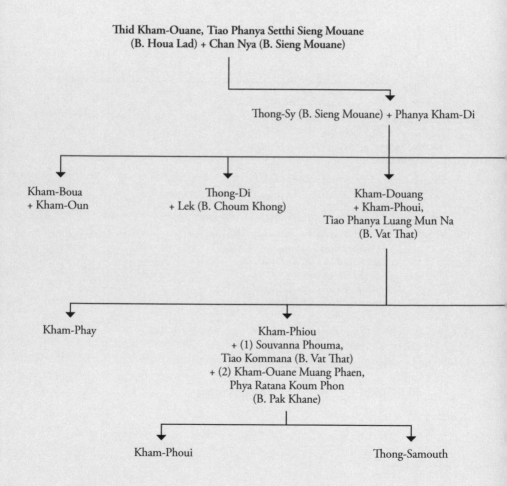

Thid Kham-Ouane, Tiao Phanya Setthi Sieng Mouane
(B. Houa Lad) + Chan Nya (B. Sieng Mouane)

Thong-Sy (B. Sieng Mouane) + Phanya Kham-Di

Kham-Boua
+ Kham-Oun

Thong-Di
+ Lek (B. Choum Khong)

Kham-Douang
+ Kham-Phoui,
Tiao Phanya Luang Mun Na
(B. Vat That)

Kham-Phay

Kham-Phiou
+ (1) Souvanna Phouma,
Tiao Kommana (B. Vat That)
+ (2) Kham-Ouane Muang Phaen,
Phya Ratana Koum Phon
(B. Pak Khane)

Kham-Phoui

Thong-Samouth

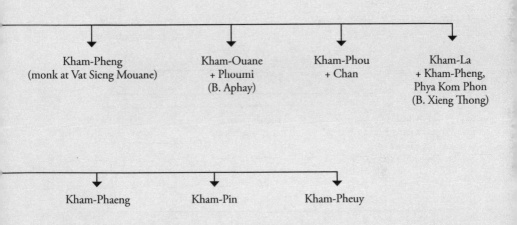

Kham-Pheng
(monk at Vat Sieng Mouane)

Kham-Ouane
+ Phoumi
(B. Aphay)

Kham-Phou
+ Chan

Kham-La
+ Kham-Pheng,
Phya Kom Phon
(B. Xieng Thong)

Kham-Phaeng

Kham-Pin

Kham-Pheuy

Family Trees

GENEALOGY OF KHAM-OUANE MUANG PHAEN

Tiao Phanya Luang Muang Saen Khaeo Khao (B. Vat That)
+ ?

↓

? + ?

- **Thong-Sy**
- **Kham-Tu**
  + Kham-Phan
  - **Kham-Peng,**
    Tiao Phanya Luang Muang Phaen
    (B. Pak Khane)
    + Douang-Kaeo (B. Vat Sop)
    - **Kham-Ouane,**
      Phya Muang Phaen
      Ratana Koumphon
      + Mom Kham-Phiou
      (B. Sieng Mouane)
      - **Kham-Phoui**
      - **Thong-Samouth**
    - **Kham-Souk**
    - **Kham-Pane**
    - **Kham-Mao**
      + Kaenchan
    - **Kham-La**
      + Bounthan
  - **Kham-Phan,**
    Phanya Tia Meun
  - **Kham-Fong**
    + Governor of Pak Beng

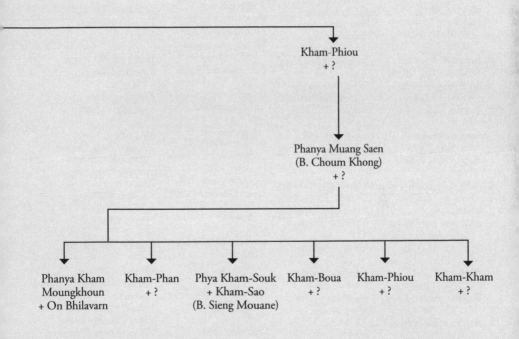

Kham-Phiou
+ ?

Phanya Muang Saen
(B. Choum Khong)
+ ?

Phanya Kham
Moungkhoun
+ On Bhilavarn

Kham-Phan
+ ?

Phya Kham-Souk
+ Kham-Sao
(B. Sieng Mouane)

Kham-Boua
+ ?

Kham-Phiou
+ ?

Kham-Kham
+ ?

Index